# BREAKING
## *the*
# Barriers

# BREAKING
## *the*
# Barriers

### OVERCOMING ADVERSITY AND
### REACHING YOUR GREATEST POTENTIAL

# JASON FRENN

New York    Boston    Nashville

Scripture quotations marked NIV are from the Holy Bible, New International Version®. Copyright © 1973, 1978, 1984 by International Bible Society. Used by permission of Zondervan Publishing House. All rights reserved.

The "NIV" and "New International Version" trademarks are registered in the United States Patent and Trademark Office by International Bible Society. Use of either trademark requires the permission of International Bible Society.

Scripture quotations marked NLT are from the Holy Bible, New Living Translation, copyright © 1996, 2004. Used by permission of Tyndale House Publishers, Inc., Wheaton, Illinois 60189. All rights reserved.

Scripture quotations marked The Message are from THE MESSAGE. Copyright © 1993, 1994, 1995, 1996, 2000, 2001, 2002. Used by permission of NavPress Publishing Group.

FaithWords
Hachette Book Group
237 Park Avenue
New York, NY 10017

Visit our Web site at www.faithwords.com.

Printed in the United States of America

First Edition: August 2009
10 9 8 7 6 5 4 3 2 1

FaithWords is a division of Hachette Book Group, Inc.
The FaithWords name and logo are trademarks of Hachette Book Group, Inc.

Library of Congress Cataloging-in-Publication Data

Frenn, Jason.
Breaking the barriers : overcoming adversity and reaching your greatest potential / by Jason Frenn.—1st ed.
p. cm.
ISBN 978-0-446-54620-1
1. Success—Religious aspects—Christianity.   2. Success—Psychological aspects.
3. Life change events—Religious aspects—Christianity.   I. Title.
BV4598.3.F74 2009
248.8'6—dc22

2008051430

*Dedicated to a great woman who continues to break barriers every day, to a great Christian who continues to grow into the image of Christ every day, to a great example who continues to love and help others find hope in Christ every day, to a great partner who continues to love me every day.*

*Dedicated to my wife, Cindee—
with all my love, admiration, respect,
and appreciation every day.*

# Contents

Acknowledgments     ix

INTRODUCTION: Are You Who You Want to Be?     xiii

CHAPTER 1: Laying a Solid Foundation     1

**PILLAR I**

**The Heart of the Father**

CHAPTER 2: Grabbing Hold of God's Heart     21

CHAPTER 3: Unleashing the Power of God's
Heart in Your Life     51

**PILLAR II**

**The Wisdom of the Son**

CHAPTER 4: Making Godly Sense     81

CHAPTER 5: Unleashing the Power of Christ's
Wisdom in Your Life     115

**PILLAR III**

**The Discipline of the Spirit**

CHAPTER 6: Peace for Your Soul     145

CHAPTER 7: Unleashing the Power of the Spirit
in Your Life     171

CONCLUSION: You Can Be Who God Wants You to Be!     203

About the Author     221

# Acknowledgments

Thank You, God the Father, for loving me enough to send Your Son and for showing me Your heart so I can truly see what it means to be made in the image of God.

Thank You, Jesus, for rescuing me from the chains of sin and for showing me Your wisdom and perspective on life. When I meditate on all You have done, I am left speechless by Your example.

Thank You, Holy Spirit, for breathing life into me and guiding me through the mountains and valleys of life. You are a great Comforter without whom we would all be without hope. Thank You for the strength to live each day with meaning and significance.

Thank you to my four ladies: Cindee, Celina, Chanel, and Jazmin. Blessed am I among women! Every day I thank the Lord for giving me the privilege of being married to such an outstanding woman and having such great daughters.

Thank you, Steve Larson, for being the first set of eyes for this book and burning the midnight oil to be the voice of reason and clarity. Thank you, Doug Brendel, for taking a close look at this manuscript. You have a gift for putting pen to paper, and I appreciate the input, edits, and guidance you invested.

Thank you, Don and Maxine Judkins, for believing in the call of God upon our lives. You have proven yourselves faithful over the years and have become great examples of what it means to serve the Lord. Thank you, Richard Larson, Channing Parks, Robert Frenn, Roberta Hart, Mike Shields, and Paul Finkenbinder, for your outstanding support. You've graciously shared your experience with the world in the pages of this book.

Thank you, Anne Horch, for seeing the potential in this work and in me. You are one of the finest and most talented editors in publishing today. God has given you a fabulous gift, and you use it for His glory. It's been my honor to work with you! Thank you, Rolf Zettersten and the entire FaithWords team, for pouring your talents into this book. You've done a fabulous job transforming a document in my computer into something people can read everywhere.

Thank you, Steve Harrison, for your friendship and for helping me communicate my message more clearly. Thank you, Roland Hinz, for going the extra distance and helping me reach a greater audience. I thank the Lord for your wholehearted dedication to reaching as many people as possible.

Thank you, Chuck Colson, for the encouraging words. You are deeply appreciated for your dedication to godliness and your commitment to Christ. Thank you, Robert H. Schuller. So many times my family needed a word of encouragement, and you were there—personally and ministerially. Thank you, Zig Ziglar, for being such a great inspiration to me from the time I sold business forms through my development as a minister. Thank you, Chip

MacGregor, for the encouragement to keep pressing on. Your talent, humility, and accessibility are very refreshing in this day and age. A special thanks to Mari-Lee Ruddy, Melodee Gruetzmacher, Steve and Karen Rutledge, Karine Rosenior, Joe Class, Rick Cortez, Rick Zorehkey, George Wood, and everyone else who took precious time to help me develop the message of this book.

# Are You Who You Want to Be?

IT WAS A WARM, dry summer evening in August 1987. My senior year at Southern California College was about to begin, and I felt sure the future would be very prosperous. As I sat in my dorm room on an old brown worn-out couch pondering the possibilities, I began to retrace my academic steps. I recalled the day I had walked onto the campus for the first time, three years before, as an idealistic seventeen-year-old focused on my mission in life. I started off as a biblical studies major and wanted to go into full-time ministry. It didn't matter whether I became a pastor, an evangelist, or a missionary, just as long as I became one of the three. After my freshman year, however, the fantasy of my Southern California ministerial life began to face a stark reality.

My dreams of serving in the ministry in Orange County were rudely interrupted by the reality of the high cost of living. Every time I pulled my 1980 baby blue Chevy Luv pickup out of the college driveway into the real world, I was surrounded by BMWs,

Mercedes Benzes, and Porsches. Prosperity and wealth were everywhere, and real-estate prices were climbing at an astronomical rate. When I began to inquire what the average salary was for ministers in the area, the answer was more than depressing.

During my sophomore year, I changed my major to history and political science. I felt such a degree would open doors for teaching in a university, practicing law, or serving in government. After a year and a half of diligent study, I sadly discovered there wasn't much more money in teaching or working for the government. Further, in order to become a lawyer, I would have to acquire a three-year law degree.

I began spreading my studies wide, making myself as diversified and marketable as possible. I took classes in business, social science, and religion. I was on course to attain a BA in history and political science, with minors in religion and business.

Serving the Lord became a distant dream. My call became a faint memory as I focused on "success." As a consequence, I began to make decisions that contradicted my Christian values. I became materialistic and focused almost entirely on attaining status. I turned my back on the call God had placed on my life, and I walked away from Him. But the saddest thing of all was: I was quickly becoming blind, not physically perhaps, but in another way.

As I sat in my dorm room reflecting on the steps I had taken, a smile came to my face. The week before, I had landed a very lucrative job. I had become a sales representative, while still in college, for an international courier company, making more money than I ever had before. I bought a whole new wardrobe, including several expensive business suits. A year before, I had traded in the old Chevy Luv for a Honda CRX. *Not bad for a start,* I thought.

I walked over to my neighbor's apartment and invited Channing to join me in checking out the Mustangs at the Ford dealership in the neighboring city of Santa Ana. It was eleven thirty at night, and the dealership was located in a rough part of town. But since most car lots leave their lights on all night, we didn't feel it would be dangerous. Besides, I was familiar with the neighborhood. We got into my year-old sports car and drove up the freeway.

We exited at the outskirts of Santa Ana and headed toward the heart of the city, taking a shortcut that led down an alley two blocks from the dealership. Unfortunately, there were hardly any streetlights, and visibility was poor. All of a sudden, two figures emerged on the right side of the alley. Not sure what their intentions were, I slowed the vehicle and continued cautiously. One of them stepped into the middle of the alleyway and threw up his hands, motioning us to stop.

Slowing to about fifteen miles per hour, we approached. The headlights gave us much better illumination. I could see that the man in our path had a cut on his forehead, and his clothes were torn. The other person was in the shadows, but it looked as if there had been a brutal fight, and I thought: *drug deal gone bad.* I had a bad feeling about it, so I accelerated and drove around them. Coming to the end of the alley, I watched in the rearview mirror as the man furiously shook his fist and screamed at me. Several hundred yards up the street was the dealership. By the time we got there, the men in the alley were several blocks away—and completely out of sight and mind.

We got out of the car and glanced across the lot. There was *my* car! I spotted it: the most impressive creation by a motor vehicle company I had ever seen. I felt like I needed to ask my friend for a moment of silence. There, parked on a ramp, was a black convertible Mustang GT. It was "high and lifted up." I was convinced angels were singing in the background. Every light in the dealership seemed to be focused on it (although at the time I was sure it gave off its own celestial glow). It looked like a black panther fast asleep, powerful in potential but resting.

We walked up to the car in slow motion. I must admit its power was seductive. It had a black leather interior, power windows, power doors, a six-speaker sound system, sixteen-inch low-profile tires, and a five-speed transmission. I looked at the sticker price and thought, *I can afford this*. I said, "Channing, this is a good day." He nodded in agreement.

In my striving for success, I had reached a pivotal moment in my life. It illustrated perfectly what I had become as a human being. I will never forget the words I muttered to myself: "Jason, if you buy this car, you will have arrived!"

Time stood still. The world froze for a few brief moments. Then the hand of God began to move.

While I was drooling over the car of my dreams, two individuals came walking up behind my CRX. It's probably not too difficult to fathom: the two people I had left in the middle of the alley. I thought, *How did they follow us? We left them a quarter of a mile ago.*

Silently, I made eye contact with my friend as if to say, "Don't say a word! Perhaps they won't notice we're here." What a ridiculous thought! Is it possible two white guys standing next to an elevated Mustang in a fully illuminated car lot in the middle of the night wouldn't be noticed?

Cars make interesting noises when you turn them off. As the engine block began to cool, my car made a *tink-tink* sound. Closing in on my vehicle, they could tell my car had just been parked, and of course, they recognized it as the same one that had left them in the middle of the alley.

They began scanning the car lot looking for the vehicle owner. Suddenly, one of them spotted us. My heart sank. Without hesitation, both of them briskly walked through the maze of cars separating us. What I thought were two black men turned out to be a husband and a wife who looked like they had just been in a gang fight. His forehead was cut, and blood covered part of his face. She looked ravaged. Their clothes were torn. Obviously they had been in some sort of altercation.

The man raised his voice in anger. "Hey, why didn't you stop when we needed you back there?"

Both my friend and I froze. I thought, *I'd better be honest with him and tell him the truth because if he pulls out a gun and shoots us, it's better to die an honest man than a liar.* Besides, I was not ready to meet my Maker. I had drifted away from my connection with God.

After a few seconds I responded, "Uh, we didn't stop in the alley because we were afraid." That was the truth, and it felt right to say it.

He stared piercingly into my eyes as if searching the deep shadows of my soul. He never blinked. Then he broke eye contact, opened his mouth with a pause, and said, "I can understand that." He extended his hand, introducing himself as if we were at a social gathering, and said, "My name is John."

I looked at his open palm and took a step back. I thought, *There is no way I am going to shake this man's hand and pretend to be friends.*

When he saw my hesitation, he exploded. "Listen," he shouted, "you can frisk me, search me, or pat me down if you want. I don't have any guns or knives. I just need your help. Now, are you going to help me or not?"

My friend and I were more than edgy. We were more than afraid. We were dealing with what seemed to be a gang member who had just lost a fight, and he was irate. We were looking for any way to calm him down.

My voice cracked when I responded to his question. "What kind of help do you need?"

He replied, "I need some money to pay for my rent, and I need to pick up my twins from the babysitter's."

Channing interrupted and said, "We'd love to help you. Where do you live?"

The man pointed to an old broken-down motel across the street. As we pulled into the parking lot, I couldn't believe my eyes. *How can they charge people money to stay in such a rat-infested slum?* I thought. Plaster was falling off the outside walls. The building looked as if it hadn't been painted in more than fifteen years. The smell was rancid, and the ceiling in some units was missing.

I stood in the doorway of their motel room while my friend went with John to the night clerk's office to pay for one night's stay. I peeked my head through the door and saw the inside of their unit. It had a very modest kitchen, a small bed, and a very small bathroom. I saw huge holes in the walls and old moldy-smelly carpeting that had probably lost its original color a decade prior to our arrival. The cupboards were bare, and the kitchen was empty. My heart went out to them. I knew they were living in a difficult situation. It was apparent they had no jobs.

Nonetheless, it was midnight, and I was getting anxious. I looked for our first possible exit, hoping to bring the night to a close. Channing gave them some additional money for food and other unforeseen needs. Then I said, "Well, we need to get back to the college."

"Hold on a minute," John said. "You still need to take me to pick up our baby twins."

Now the last thing I wanted was to be this guy's private chauffeur in Santa Ana on a Friday night. Who would want to take a drive in one of the most dangerous neighborhoods in Southern California at midnight? Besides, it didn't seem right. It was too risky, and too dangerous. But he insisted.

He said, "Do you have kids?"

"No," I replied.

"Well, when you do, you'll understand you can't abandon them. Please help me. Take me to them so I can bring them home to their mother."

I hesitated and looked down before reluctantly agreeing. *Besides, my friend is with me,* I thought. *It can't be* that *dangerous.* So we got into the CRX, which was a two-seater. Since there was no place for John to sit, he had to sit on the emergency brake, sandwiched between Channing and me. Just two blocks into our journey, we entered a tougher part of the city, where much of the gang activity took place. It was dark inside the car, and the streetlights didn't give off much illumination.

I strained to see with my peripheral vision what our passenger was doing with his hands, which were tucked into his lap. Then, breaking a very awkward moment of silence, he said, "I'm going to tell you something, man." I thought, *Oh Lord, I should have taken him up on his offer.* I should have frisked him back at the car lot.

He said, "God is going to bless you for what you have done tonight."

"Come again?" I replied.

"You heard me. God is going to bless you for what you have done."

Then he turned to me and said, "My mom was a missionary to Africa. She preached the gospel to many people and depended on God for all she had. If I learned one thing from her example, it's this: you can't serve God and money. You will love one and hate the other, or you will despise one and worship the other. No one can serve two masters. I would rather live as a poor man and struggle from day to day. I would rather depend on God for my daily provisions than live in the rat race of Southern California. Yes, the Lord will bless you for what you have done for us tonight."

When we arrived at the sitter's, John ran inside and discovered that someone had taken the twins back to his motel while we were in route. We turned around and headed back.

After we dropped him off at the motel, Channing and I continued on our way back to the college. As we drove past the car dealership, I noticed the Mustang didn't look as tempting as it had before. It wasn't "high and lifted up." It had no celestial glow. And there weren't any angels singing in the background.

When we reached the campus, we went our separate ways. Once again I found myself sitting on the same old brown couch. This time, I began to ponder something more significant. Instead of fantasizing about money and attaining social status, I had to ask myself what was truly important. To the question "Are you who you want to be?" my answer was a sobering no. And that forced me to look past the emptiness of materialism and ask the one question that, sooner or later, everyone asks. . . . Why am I here?

I do not come from a religious home. My parents were separated when I was three and divorced when I was nine, and my mom remarried someone who was thirty-two years older than her. For a time, he produced NC-17 videos. Between my three parents there were eight divorces. My dad made ends meet as a bartender for more than fifty years, and my mom struggled with alcoholism. As a teenager, I saw my father for a few hours twice a month.

When I was fifteen, I met Someone very significant. He helped me through those difficult times. He believed in me when no one else would. He helped me when no one else could. And He gave me hope when there was none to be found. His name was Jesus, and He came to me when life seemed to have no meaning. After two years, I went to college to prepare myself to serve Him in full-time ministry. But because of the pressures of the world, I lost my focus. I lost my direction. I lost my way and found myself living behind barriers. Ironically, in my pursuit of financial freedom and material wealth, I had become a slave to the love of money. I had become barricaded behind its barriers. I turned my back on the one Person who gave me life and meaning.

There in the dorm room in August 1987, I asked Him to forgive me for walking away. I prayed a simple prayer: "Lord, help me set my life straight." The God of heaven responded. He forgave me and helped me make things right. As a result, I figured out why I am here.

I regained my direction. I found my godly reason for living. My path became clear. My vision became focused once again. Years later, I have proclaimed the gospel at more than fifty crusades and ministered in more than twelve countries. I am very grateful for all God has allowed me to see and do. God helps us overcome every challenge that separates us from becoming all we are destined to be.

In the pages of this book, you will find the insights that have helped me break barriers and overcome adversity. If you make the commitment to read this book and refer back to it from time to time, you too will experience great victory in breaking barriers, overcoming adversity, and reaching your greatest potential.

But keep in mind: many of us resist change. Often change comes only when the pain of staying the same becomes greater than the pain of change itself. I might never have thought of changing directions in my life if not for my experience that night at the car lot.

Now you have a decision to make. Are you ready for change? Are you ready to break the barriers? Are you ready to break the chains holding you captive? Are you ready to move on to your greatest potential? I trust your answer is an overwhelming yes. You can be who God wants you to be! You can break the barriers, overcome adversity, and reach your greatest potential. With God, all things are possible!

As we set out to overcome the barriers that hold us back, we need to address three basic questions. Answering these three questions will help us begin the journey on the right foot.

## THE THREE QUESTIONS OF LIFE

### Why?

Do you know *why* you are here? Does your life have purpose? I am convinced it does. This is what motivated me to write this book for you. There is a great purpose behind the creation of your life. You are unique. No one is like you.

So let me help you discover the answer to the question "Why am I here?" You are not here by mistake. Your life is not an accident, nor do you exist because of some random evolutionary chance. You are here by design. And you are here on earth for a reason.

I believe you embody a divine purpose with eternal value. This is a fundamental truth whether you are conscious of it or not. Someone purposefully intended for you to be born, and that Person wants you to have a meaningful and significant life. That Person is God. Yes, I believe in God. And more important, He believes in you. You have purpose because God created you. He wants and has destined you to be here. You are very important to Him.

God created us for His pleasure and wants to have fellowship with us as His sons and daughters (see Ephesians 1:4–7). This means God wants to have a relationship with you. That's why you are here. Today, He wants you to pray, worship, meditate, and study. He wants you to walk with Him, learn from Him, and communicate with Him. You can be assured that nothing in all creation can separate you from His love. Nothing can smother His desire to have a relationship with you (see Romans 8:38–39). That's how important you are to Him.

## What?

Are there times when you feel disconnected from God's purpose for your life? Do you feel you are achieving nothing of eternal value? Do you lack direction? Have you ever struggled with the question "What am I doing with my life?" An uncertainty lurks over us when we sense we are achieving very little of lasting value. We may feel as if our lives are going nowhere.

What *are* you doing with your life?

If these challenges have bounced around in your head, I want you to know I have stood in your shoes. I know how you feel. Many times, I have shopped for the secrets of success. I have longed to discover the golden nugget that would liberate me from the barriers preventing me from reaching my greatest potential. I have watched late-night infomercials, looking for answers with credit card in hand, seeking someone who could give me guidance. Like many, I have thumbed through the pages of self-help books, intensely searching for the one missing element that has eluded me for years. I have attended seminars and conferences and talked to the best of the best. After years of studying the Scriptures and talking with people who are the finest in their fields, I have come to an amazing discovery. I will share this discovery with you. But first, we must identify the barriers that hold many people back.

What area of your life needs to experience a breakthrough? If you could state it in one sentence, what would be the greatest obstacle you face? Is it a challenge to your health or weight? Is it a challenge with your family, career, or finances? When you look in the mirror, do you like what you see? Are you being held captive, going around in circles, feeling dissatisfied? Until you identify those areas keeping you paralyzed, finding the solutions will be difficult. So dig deep. Soul-search. Ask yourself, *What are my barriers?*

Picking up this book is a step on the road to victory. I have made the journey, and I have talked to thousands of others who have made this journey as well. The pages ahead contain some of their stories, which I have included to help, motivate, and inspire you. As those I will describe have done, you can embrace your divine purpose, identify your barriers, and develop the strength to permanently move beyond them.

## How?

Ah, now this is the question everyone wants answered. "How do I break the barriers? How do I become a better Christian, parent, or spouse? How do I walk in God's will and advance in my career, make more money, or lose weight? How do I make the quantum leap? How do I become all I am destined to be without losing my soul in the process?" I have good news for you, my friend. This book will help you find answers to these questions. It will give you practical solutions. It will help you form proactive habits as a step toward creating a life full of meaning and significance. As a result you will become all you are destined to be.

Some of the answers you discover might not be what you want to hear. They might not tickle your ears. But you will find real answers and real solutions. You will discover the true essence of a meaningful and significant life, a life that breaks barriers and functions at its greatest capacity. What you will discover in the pages of this book will change your life.

## SO, WHAT'S IN IT FOR YOU?

At this moment, I imagine you scanning the introduction of this book in the aisle of a bookstore. Perhaps you are at an airport between flights and have stepped into a travel shop. Maybe a friend gave the book to you. There you stand after whisking through the first few pages, asking yourself: *So, what's in it for me?* Maybe you're asking yourself, *What does this book have to offer that millions of others don't?* What a great question! It's the right one to ask. Now it's up to me to answer it.

Over the past eight years, I have spoken to crowds totaling more than two million people. I have counseled thousands and prayed for tens of thousands in twelve countries on two continents. I've hosted a live radio program, interviewing people who have been transformed from survival mode to lives that thrive. I lived in Central America and traveled extensively throughout a region once torn by natural disasters and civil wars. My eyes have seen the miraculous. I have seen God put broken lives back together. I have seen people rise from the ashes of total ruin and surpass their greatest dreams. How? They teamed together with the One who created them with purpose and destiny.

I have seen thousands of lives transformed. Regardless of your race, age, gender, socioeconomic status, or educational achievement, following the principles in this book will reap unimaginable benefits. I have never seen them fail.

Perhaps you feel others look happier and more fulfilled than you. Is your life plagued by monotonous and meaningless patterns? If this is the case, you need help. And I want to offer a helping hand.

My desire is that you become all God destined you to be. I want you to reach your greatest potential, exceeding all dreams, aspirations, and expectations. Even more, I want you to discover true meaning and significance. Most important, I want you to discover the power of a relationship with God that will set you free from the chains that have kept you in bondage. This book is the key to a new life that will help you reach your greatest potential. Your greatest days are ahead, and the benefits will be immeasurable. That's what's in it for you!

In the next chapter, we'll focus on three essential steps that will give us a healthy perspective for our journey. Then, once we've laid that foundation, we will develop the heart of this book: the three pillars. These three pillars—the heart of the Father, the wisdom of the Son, and the discipline of the Spirit—are essential for a life filled with meaning and significance. If you're serious about becoming all God has destined you to be, turn the page, and together we'll begin the journey of breaking down the barriers that are holding you back.

# BREAKING
## *the*
# Barriers

CHAPTER 1

# *Laying a Solid Foundation*

HEAVY RAINS and intermittent fog made driving the "Mount of Death" difficult and scary for missionary Richard Larson. He was following a passage through one of the most treacherous mountains in Central America at nearly eleven thousand feet, but he couldn't see it—there were no streetlights, the rain was coming in sheets, and the only way he knew he was still on the road was by watching the taillights of a large truck thirty yards ahead. Where the truck went, Richard followed. Suddenly, without warning, the taillights disappeared. After a few seconds they reappeared. Somewhat puzzled, Richard continued following for several seconds and then, alone in his car, he heard a voice say, "*Stop!*"

Immediately, he slammed on the brakes. Brought to a halt at the precise location where the truck lights momentarily disappeared, he was astonished by what he saw. His vehicle had stopped just short of a precipice. The entire road had disappeared. The heavy tropical rains had pounded the mountains and caused a huge landslide. A thirty-yard section of the road vanished into a

1

huge ravine that continued down a forty-five-degree slope several hundred feet below. Apparently the truck driver had veered sharply to the left, where an older provisional section of the road remained against the mountainside and led around the washout. For a few brief moments his taillights had vanished from Larson's view. Because of the mysterious voice the missionary heard that night in 1966, his life was altered forever.

Today, Richard and Janice Larson are still missionaries and have accomplished more than the pages of this book could contain. Their oldest daughter, Melodee, along with her husband, Larry, served as missionaries to Mexico City for more than fifteen years and have had a great impact on the entire country. The Larsons' oldest son, Mark, is the vice president of a tour bus company that chauffeurs celebrities of every walk of life. He was privileged to drive President George W. Bush in the campaigns leading up to two presidential elections. Cindee is their third daughter. She is an ordained minister, general presbyter, a children's crusade evangelist, and a mother of three. She happens to be my wife. Steve is the youngest son. He graduated from law school at the top of his class and worked as a law clerk for the Federal Circuit Court of Appeals in Washington, D.C., hearing cases from all over the country. He is currently working for a prestigious law firm in Newport Beach, California.

What might have happened to the lives mentioned above if Richard Larson had not listened to the voice telling him to stop? What might happen to your life or the lives of those you care about if you do not heed the signs in your path? Perhaps God is trying to get your attention. Maybe He is telling you to stop. Why? Because He wants to give you a clear mission and keep you from being derailed. God wants your direction to be crystal clear and has no desire for you to crash into a ravine. Therefore, it is important for you to choose God's divine course, to make His course your own.

Richard Larson had one moment to change his direction, and he seized it. When such a moment to change your direction presents itself, it's imperative that you respond immediately. Perhaps the moment for change is here, now.

This chapter focuses on three important steps that prepare us for the journey. These steps include accepting Christ as our guide and source for direction, accepting responsibility for our own decisions, and accepting the fact that God loves us unconditionally. Completing these steps will help us lay the right foundation upon which we will build three essential pillars. Toward the end of the chapter, we'll take a brief look at these pillars and how they empower us to break the barriers we face. Then, in the chapters that follow, we'll explore each pillar in depth.

## THE JOURNEY STARTS HERE

The first step in laying a solid foundation to break the barriers, regardless of what they may be, is to have the right guide. There is nothing worse for a navigator than to have the wrong coordinates. Or imagine having the wrong map. Our ability to navigate the turbulences of life is vital, but we commonly try to do so without proper instrumentation. We need a compass. It must be accurate. It must be reliable. It must be fail-safe. Why? Because our lives depend on it.

A few years ago, my wife and I attained our scuba-diving certifications. As divers, we must be able to navigate in zero visibility through strong currents as well as at night. This is possible only with an accurate compass. A good compass can guide you through the most turbulent storms, treacherous terrain, and foggy conditions. It always points north.

The Bible is the main compass of life. It is the most reliable guidance device in the history of the world. No book has helped as many people move in the right direction as God's inspired masterpiece. It's the playbook of life. The Bible contains God's inspired spiritual laws and guidelines that help us live healthy and godly lives. It too always points north. And it will be our compass throughout our journey together as we break the barriers preventing us from moving forward.

## CHRIST: TRUE NORTH

Christ is the central figure of the New Testament, and many of the prophets of the Old Testament foretold His coming. When the authorities of His day asked Him who He was, He responded in John 14:6, "I am the way and the truth and the life. No one comes to the Father except through me" (NIV). Christ is the way, the truth, and the life. The only way to get to heaven is through Him. He is the door. He knows the way. He is the perfect guide.

In my travels around the world, I have counseled many people. I have discovered many trying to navigate life with a broken compass. The way they see the world is contorted. They are confused and disoriented. Lost and vulnerable, their compasses carry them sideways or in circles.

In some cases people have confessed to me they wish they had never been born. Or perhaps they envy the lives of others. When they look in the mirror, they are not pleased by what they see. They do not feel satisfied with the way they are developing as people.

Because of their seemingly powerless state, they have feelings of helplessness, depression, alienation, and loneliness. Eventually these feelings bubble over, especially when the day comes to a close. When the room is filled with silence, when all the noise of the day stops, when no one else is awake, that is when the pain becomes overwhelming. That is when the anguish overshadows them. Negative self-talk takes over. It begins to pound in their heads.

At such a moment, we all need relief. In the midst of the storm, we need direction. Sooner or later, we all need a compass. Sooner or later, we all need help. Sooner or later, we all need God. When we think life has no purpose and isn't worth living, God steps into the picture and offers to become our compass and guide. When the turbulence of life overwhelms us, He shines His love upon us and parts the clouds. Just when you think you are not worth anything, God says you are worth the price of the death of His Son.

Turning your life over to Christ is the first step in the right direction. Allow Him to be the compass and guide you need. Allow Him to give you the tools to navigate your life. If you accept the offer God makes you, the light will shine again. You will come out of the tunnel. The clouds will part. The turbulence will subside. You will break the barriers. Remember, a life connected to the right mission has purpose. Knowing Christ gives you the right mission.

## THE BUCK STOPS HERE!

The second step in laying a solid foundation to break the barriers is to accept personal responsibility. This is where many of us fail in our quest to move ahead. Instead of accepting responsibility, many would prefer to blame others for their problems. We have become a society that casts fault. For instance, during an election each political party blames the other for the unacceptable conditions of the nation. Children blame their parents for raising them too strictly. Parents blame schools for poor education. Teachers blame the districts for insufficient funding. People blame governments. Governments blame other governments. And sooner or later, everyone blames God. We have become a world of experts at passing the buck, evading responsibility as if it were a disease.

Take being overweight, for example. This is a common struggle for many people. For twelve years, I was sixty pounds overweight, and my weight is something I continue to monitor very closely. I ate more than I should have because I couldn't manage the anxieties that haunted me.

If you struggle with your weight, I want you to know that I understand. Food is different from any other issue we may face. Unlike narcotics, cigarettes, and alcohol, we need food to survive.

To make matters worse, advertisers constantly bombard us with images to entice us into buying their products. When the forces of advertising, hunger, and emotional insomnia converge, it's no wonder so many people struggle with their weight. There are many different explanations for an overweight condition. However, we cannot shift our responsibility to something or someone else. When all is said and done, we are the ones who make the choice to purchase the product, open our mouths, and indulge.

If overeating is your barrier, you must make the choice to overcome it. You must take responsibility. Don't wait for someone to change you. Don't wait for the emotional chaos to stop before you take your first step. Don't put your hope in some miracle pill to give you a perfect body. Don't wait until your anxiety subsides or you *feel* that your life is in order. Choose to break the barrier and learn to work through the issues underlying your struggle.

Ask God for help, and with His help, you will overcome. Remember, regardless of the reason for your struggle, in order for you to break free from your destructive patterns, you must take responsibility, partner with God, and develop the self-discipline to take care of your body. Take responsibility today for your condition and ask God to help you live a healthy life. Shifting the blame hurts only one person: you.

The same can be said for those who are buried in debt. People blame their employers for not paying them "what they are worth." Or they blame their spouses for being compulsive spenders. Instead of being responsible and living within a budget, they cast blame on others for their financial problems. In their failure to get ahead, they blame interest rates, financial markets, or even the president. Humans are constantly looking for scapegoats for their failure to reach their financial goals.

Marriage is not exempt from the blame game. Many times, I have heard wives complain they are not content because their husbands do not make them happy. They assume their husbands exist for this sole purpose. Husbands fire back by claiming they are neglected, and as a result give themselves permission to engage in extramarital activities.

Instead of playing the blame game, spouses should recognize they cannot depend on each other for their own happiness. None of the marriage vows I've read state one spouse exists to make the other happy. Instead, spouses should love and cherish each other. When the dust settles, each person in a marriage is responsible for his or her own happiness.

It's amazing how our society blames parents for the errors their children commit when they become adults. If someone turns out to be a lawbreaker or a menace to society, the first thing we do is point to the parents. It's true parents carry much of the burden, and children must be guided. We can see the importance of nurturing and guiding children in their development toward adulthood. But when they are grown, they are responsible for their own decisions and actions. Many come from bad homes and turn out to be extraordinary people. Others come from great homes and turn out to be horrific people. Ultimately, the individual who acts is responsible. Just because people were raised in a home where there was violence, neglect, or abuse does not mean they must repeat the same behavior as adults. If they do, it is because they choose to do so.

The same tension exists in the workplace, where the boss may be seen as someone who exists for the sole purpose of standing in the way of the employees and saying no to every request made. Or perhaps sabotage by colleagues is perceived as the reason a promotion or a pay raise wasn't granted. Certain coworkers seem to be given favor while others remain stuck in a meaningless rut without an exit. The finger of blame and responsibility is always pointing at others.

At the end of the day, we need to ask the question, "Am I reaching my greatest potential?" Is your honest answer yes or no? I have some news: If we want to become all we are destined to be, we need to stop blaming others for our condition. We must take responsibility for our own lives.

Think about it for a moment. If you want to marry someone, no one else can marry that person on your behalf. No one can drink water for you. No one can lose weight for you. No one can build muscle for your body. No one can eat right so your body receives nutrition. No one can study so your brain will be filled with information. Can anyone breathe for someone else? Can anyone exercise for someone else? Can anyone sleep for someone else? No. Only we can do these things for ourselves. Therefore, if you want to overcome and become all you were destined to be, stop blaming others for your lack of advancement. Take responsibility for your life. Be responsible for the choices you have made. The buck stops here!

## GOD'S LOVE WILL LEAD YOU THERE

The third step in laying a solid foundation to break the barriers is to accept that God loves you unconditionally. This is a simple truth: God loves you and wants the best for your life. Why? Because you are His child. You have been created in His image. What parent wants the worst for his or her child? What parent wants his or her children to suffer or stay stagnant? What parent hopes his or her child will turn out to be a loser? As parents, we want our children to grow, be healthy, and reach their greatest potential.

This is what the Bible says about you in Galatians 3:26: "You are all sons of God through faith in Christ Jesus" (NIV). Deuteronomy 23:5 states, "The LORD your God would not listen to Balaam but turned the curse into a blessing for you, because the LORD your God loves you" (NIV). Jesus states in John 16:27: "The Father himself loves you because you have loved me and have believed that I came from God" (NIV). Zechariah 2:8 states, "Whoever touches you touches the apple of his eye" (NIV).

My wife and I have three lovely daughters. Each one is unique. Each one is special. Each one is wonderful in her own way. They are not perfect, but when I look at them, my heart cannot help but melt. When they look at me with their big eyes and innocent expressions, they are no less than the apple of my eye. Why? Because they are my girls. They are part of me. A bond exists between us. Whether my girls are conscious of that fact makes no difference. Whether they are aware they have been formed in my image is of no consequence. We have a union no one can erase. This is an irrefutable fact. The same is true between God and us.

Genesis 1:26 quotes God as saying, "Let us make man in our image, in our likeness, and let them rule over the fish of the sea and the birds of the air, over the livestock, over all the earth, and over all the creatures that move along the ground" (NIV). Part of our genetic code comes from God. We were created in His image. Because of this bond, He loves us. He wants us to grow and flourish. We are His offspring, and in the same way that a child reaching his potential is a positive reflection of his parents, our progress in breaking barriers is a positive reflection of our heavenly Father. Consequently, He wants us to move beyond the challenges that keep us from fulfilling His divine plan for our lives. He wants us to break barriers.

## THE THREE PILLARS

In order to overcome any problem, obstacle, challenge, or barrier, we must have the right values (the heart of the Father), judgment (the wisdom of the Son), and strength (the discipline of the Spirit). These are the three pillars that form a blessed and significant life, a life that reaches its potential. These pillars break barriers, no matter how large or difficult. They open a new world filled with significance, meaning, and potential.

These pillars are not a three-step program. Each one is essential and seamlessly connected to the others. If we embrace only one or two of the three, we leave a gaping hole.

The first pillar is the heart of the Father, a heart of integrity, godliness, virtue, and decency. In essence, it is the character of God the Father. This is the moral compass, or godly direction, we need to give us the right mission and help us align ourselves with *why* we are here. I will discuss the first pillar in depth in chapters 2 and 3.

The second pillar is the wisdom of the Son, which gives us the ability to be good people and to make good decisions in harmony with our mission. With godly wisdom based upon the mind of Christ, we judge every decision we make in light of our God-given mission. Many people are good, but few are good and wise. Wisdom helps us decide *what* we should do. Chapters 4 and 5 deal with the power of God's wisdom to break barriers.

The third pillar is the discipline of the Spirit, which supplies us with the strength necessary to put into practice good decisions based on godly character and godly wisdom. Many of us recognize what the right course of action is but don't have the energy and discipline to carry it out. The Holy Spirit gives us the power to complete the *how* to. Chapters 6 and 7 focus on this third pillar.

These three pillars together form what we need for a meaningful and significant life. And a meaningful and significant life is not wrapped in materialism, superficiality, or a false sense of success. True purpose, significance, and success come only when we live in harmony with God's divine purpose for our lives. As we fulfill God's purpose and live in the circle of godly direction, godly wisdom, and godly strength, we cannot help but break the barriers that try to hold us back.

Keep in mind: the principles we discuss must be adhered to in order to succeed. We cannot take a shortcut through them or find some way around them. I wouldn't encourage anyone to continue reading as if this is a three-step self-help book aimed at making him or her the most successful person on the planet in thirty days. Reaching your greatest potential isn't easy. It's hard work!

So where's the starting point? You can start right here, right now, just as you are. The following story illustrates that no matter who you are, where you come from, or what challenges you face, God loves you and will help you overcome the toughest barriers. He is your greatest ally!

## WHAT ARE YOU DOING WITH YOUR LIFE?

In December 2003, I received a call from my crusade coordinator. He said he had spoken to a young man who wanted to come in and tell us his story. I asked if he knew anything about the young man. He replied, "All I know is, you'll want to hear this!"

When the young man came to our studios for the interview, he introduced himself as John. His interview with us lasted over an hour. I sat him down in a chair as our soundman connected the microphone and prepared the audio feed. I checked the camera and made a few lighting adjustments. We began recording. I remember he was sweating, probably because he had never been interviewed on-camera before. I handed him a towel to wipe his forehead. As I thought about what my crusade coordinator had said to me, I noticed the young man taking a few deep breaths. Looking back later, I realized my coordinator was right. What I heard that day had a powerful impact on my life. To this day, I consider the ministry fortunate to have recorded his testimony on video.

He handed the towel back to me and nodded. I said, "If you're ready, let's get started." I counted down from three, pointed to him, and said, "You're on."

He replied, "Uh, where do you want me to begin?"

I smiled and said, "Why not start from the womb?" He chuckled. That was the icebreaker he needed.

During his interview, which contained graphic details of the sexual, physical, and emotional abuse he endured from his parents, John shared how he fell into a life of drug addiction and alcoholism by the age of ten. After five years of unruly and unsupervised living in the streets of Central America, he stumbled into one of our open-air campaigns and committed his life to Christ. For nine long months, John tried to leave his old life behind while attending a local church. But he never felt understood. He never felt accepted. The change in his life lasted only a short season.

Once again, he turned to drugs and the destructive patterns he'd embraced before. At eighteen, he moved in with a young woman who had two children from a previous relationship. One day, he came home early from work and found her in bed with another man, which resulted in an explosive altercation. The police arrested him and took him to jail.

Unfortunately, life behind bars was not conducive to his spiritual growth. Old habits are hard to break. When John got out, he turned to two of his lifelong companions: drugs and alcohol.

One day, he got up and went through his normal routine of firing up his pipe and smoking a rock of crack. Later that afternoon, he wandered the streets, oblivious and high, and stumbled onto our crusade lot. As he listened to the message, pondering the decisions he had made up to that point, he asked himself, *What am I doing with my life?*

Then he heard the words of Christ as I read John 8:36: "If the Son sets you free, you will be free indeed" (NIV). At that moment, he made a choice. He decided to turn the reins of his life over to the Lord. He embraced God as his compass in life. John went forward in a sea of five thousand people during the invitation and asked God for forgiveness. Once again, he discovered God's love and realized that Christ died for his sins. This time, things would be different. He chose God's direction for his life.

In the weeks following the campaign, someone in a local church introduced John to the leader of a small group for those who came from similar backgrounds. He decided to attend. It was the first time anyone had genuinely reached out to him. Tears welled up in his eyes as he gratefully accepted the offer. Week after week, John faithfully went to the meetings. After several months, he went to a weekend retreat with 120 young people who, like him, struggled with addictions and came from abusive homes. That weekend turned out to be the most important one of his life.

The counselors prayed with him and guided him through the process of dealing with his painful and abusive past. They helped him pray through his feelings of rejection, abandonment, and alienation. Most important, they helped him forgive those who had hurt him.

Since June 2003, he has faithfully attended his small group without any relapse into drugs. In 2005, he was recruited as a leader and today leads a small group. He has become a new man!

When he finished telling me his story, silence permeated the room. After a few moments, I asked him if I could use his testimony. He replied, "That's why I came. I came to help as many people as I could. You can share this with anyone you think would benefit from my story."

During his time with us, not once did the young man blame anyone for his problems. He owned up to every mistake. He took responsibility for his own actions. He recognized God's love. He recognized God's direction and acquired a new compass. He repented. He asked for and received God's forgiveness. He broke through some of the most difficult barriers possible and continues in the process of becoming an outstanding human being. Since 2003, John has made something of his life.

Now, if a young man who was physically, sexually, and emotionally abused, who faced poverty and rejection, can resist blaming others for his tragic life, can we find the strength to do the same? Too many blame others for their problems. Instead, be a man! Be a woman! Own up to your life and take responsibility. Ask yourself, *What am I doing with my life?*

I learned something from John. I discovered that in God's eyes no vice is unconquerable. No life is unredeemable. No heart is unchangeable. No act is unpardonable. No barrier is unbreakable. I discovered that with God's help anyone can change. Anyone can be restored. Anyone can be healed. Anyone can be set free. No storm lasts forever. No mountain is too high. No wall is too thick. No obstacle is too difficult in light of God's power to help us break the barriers.

So as we take the next step together, embrace this notion: God loves you and has a purpose for your life. He provides His Son as revealed in the Bible as a compass and guide. He asks you to be responsible for your actions and the decisions you have made (see Romans 14:12). Although difficult times may present themselves, you will overcome, and the Lord will strengthen you. Because you were made in His image, He loves you and provides the necessary means for you to reach your greatest potential.

Thus far, we've learned three wonderful lessons for the journey. We can depend on Christ and the Bible as perfect guides. We don't have to keep blaming others for our disappointments. We've learned that the Creator of the universe loves us unconditionally. Now, are you ready to unleash God's power against your barriers? Are you ready to see His hand move? I trust you are!

In the next two chapters, I will share with you how to overcome your barriers with the power of God's heart. You will discover the importance of having a heart of integrity, godliness, virtue, and decency and how these attributes are the necessary starting point for overcoming life's challenges. As a result of grabbing hold of the heart of God, you'll be well on your way to a life filled with meaning and significance!

I am going to ask something of you. I trust it will not make you feel uncomfortable. We are going to close our time with a moment of meditation with the Lord. Of all the lessons we have learned, this is by far the most important. Prayer and meditation are the door through which we approach the first pillar. Therefore, say the following words as a prayer and dedication as we break the barriers together:

*Dear God, thank You for the opportunity to live. You gave me the wonderful gift of life. You gave me a divine purpose and a breathtaking destiny. Help me to make the most of my existence. And help me to overcome those obstacles that have kept my life in chains. I want to reach my greatest potential, and partnering with You is the only way I can. I realize difficult times may present themselves. Nonetheless, You will direct me through them, because You love me.*

*I ask You for guidance. I ask You to be my compass. Point me in the right direction. Lord Jesus, I need You. I need You to come into my life and transform my mind and the way I see things. I ask You to forgive me for anything I have done that is offensive to You or those in my life. Come into my heart and become Lord over my life. Give me a humble heart, one that isn't filled with pride. I commit myself to You and ask for the strength to embrace the principles outlined in this book.*

*I now embark upon the adventure of getting to know*

*You. Most important, I commit myself to whatever You ask of me during this process of change. Help me to be strong, obedient, and open to Your change for my life. Make Yourself real to me with each passing day. I pray these things in Christ's name. Amen.*

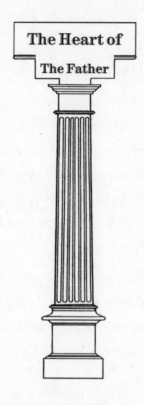

The Heart of
The Father

Right Values

| Moral Compass | Kindness | Gentleness |
| Love | Faithfulness | Self-Control |
| Patience | Joy | Godly Mission |

## The Heart of the Father

*God the Father is filled with compassion and beautiful attributes. He has always sought to bring redemption, health, and goodness to humanity. In times of trial and difficulty, His heart acts as a moral compass, guiding us through the storms of life. The heart of the Father is the first pillar in our quest to break the barriers that separate us from becoming all God has destined us to be.*

*When we establish a heart that is godly and pure, we will experience love, patience, kindness, faithfulness, joy, gentleness, healthy self-esteem, and self-control. This is the first step toward a life filled with meaning and significance.*

CHAPTER 2

# Grabbing Hold of God's Heart

EASTER BREAK was always a great time of year for me. A week off from school without any homework provided a fertile time of fun and entertainment. My mom went off to work each of the five days, and my father would check in on me from time to time. The year I turned eleven, Holy Week was no different. I felt free from burden and stress.

At the time, I was playing hockey in a kids' league. One day I set up my hockey net in our carport. Using a tennis ball, I practiced my hockey shots, trying to improve my accuracy. After several hours, it started to rain and I went inside. The rain was problematic to practicing, and besides, playing by myself was not much fun. I wasn't allowed to have friends over when my mom wasn't home. The next day when Mom was at work, I set up the net again, but this time, my neighbor asked if he could join me. I didn't think it would be a problem since he wouldn't be going inside the house. So I agreed. Little did I know my concurrence was part of a formula for disaster.

Instead of practicing our ability to score goals, we decided to play a one-on-one tournament. The little carport was only big enough for my mom's 1969 Volkswagen Bug. It hardly had the space for a hockey game. The ramifications of a potential catastrophe were not the foremost things on my mind, however. I was determined to win at all costs, especially against a neighbor two years older than me who had beaten me at almost every other sport.

Occasionally, the ball would land in the mud where the rain had pounded the soil for several hours the day before. Pulling it from the sludge and putting it back in play was my second mistake. After about six or seven times of pulling the ball from the mud, the carport started to take on a whole new look. It was as if we were repainting the carport with a bouncing sponge soaked to capacity with a brownish-black substance.

The carport walls were made of stucco, and the vaulted ceiling was freshly painted white wood. As time went on, the game became more fierce and violent. The ball began to ricochet from ceiling to wall to floor. Like a Super Ball exploding off a concrete surface, the drenched round hockey puck left its mark at least several hundred times. Each time the ball left a huge splat on the wall, the spray hit us in the face as well. My mom's beautiful newly painted white carport soon began to resemble the house in *The Cat in the Hat* after the arrival of Thing One and Thing Two.

There was a bit of good news in all this. When the afternoon was finished, I had won the tournament. I was the victor. I was the champion. It was one of the first times I had ever beat the eighth grader in *any* sport. Although he went home with his head hung low in defeat, he was lucky enough to avoid the wrath about to come home in a light blue VW Bug.

We usually went out to dinner on Friday nights, and I wanted to take a shower before my mom came home. So I started to break down the net and put away my hockey sticks. I never once stopped to think about the consequences of our actions. I hardly noticed the hundreds of polka-dot splat patterns left behind. Nor did I think about what my mom might say when she saw them.

At 6:30 p.m., darkness had settled over Southern California. She pulled her car into the carport and got out. Looking puzzled at first, she gazed at the walls for a brief few moments. She came into the house and said, "Jason, were you playing in the carport?" Time to face the facts: our hockey tournament had left obvious evidence of horseplay—in fact, it looked like a miniature war zone, and although my first instinct was to dismiss Mom's question, she wouldn't let it go, and my attempts to hide the truth were futile.

I said, "Well, um, yes, I was playing. But I was just practicing."

"What were you practicing?" she asked with a serious tone.

"Hockey."

Without a word she returned to the carport to inspect the damage more closely.

About ten seconds passed before the first confirmation of my imminent doom came with an authoritative scream. "Jason, get out here now!" Once I was outside, she demanded, "How in the world did you get mud all over the walls and ceiling? There are round spots everywhere."

"The ball did it."

"What do you mean, the *ball* did it?"

"We were playing hockey, and the ball bounced against the wall."

"Wait a minute!" she exclaimed. "Who is 'we'?"

Oops. Now the cat was out of the bag. We had arrived at the point of no return. Might as well make my funeral arrangements.

"Me and Scott . . ."

"You mean to tell me you had a friend over here when neither your father nor I was home?" she interrogated. "I can't believe it. I just can't believe it. Get in the house!"

"Aren't we going out to dinner?" I timidly inquired.

She looked at me with eyes of steel. If looks could kill, I would have been incinerated that very instant back in 1977 by the laser beams rocketing from her blue eyes. She gritted her teeth and growled, "What do you think?"

Most of the time, my baby blue eyes and curly brown hair helped me get out of any mess. Not this time. No, this time my goose was cooked. My guilt was apparent, and the evidence was overwhelming. There was nowhere to hide and no one to protect me.

She called my dad, who was tending bar that night. "Bob, you won't believe what your son did today!" She explained everything that had happened. Unfortunately, she left out the part about my *winning* the hockey tournament, which might have helped my case from my dad's perspective. Of course, considering how mad she was, it made sense she would forget that part.

During the hockey game, it never occurred to me that the exciting pastime was going to cause me big trouble in the near future. It was obvious the ball was tracking mud everywhere. It was well known to me that friends were forbidden at the house when my parents weren't there. Obviously, ruining the new paint job would infuriate my mom. I managed to ignore all that and enjoy the game—with no thought of the cost.

Yet my parents never disciplined me for the incident. My only punishment was hearing my mom cry tears of frustration over my disobedience and failure to follow the rules. Knowing the pain I had caused her was enough punishment for me. She began to clean up but was unable to complete even a third of the task. The next day I helped her scrub and clean the walls and ceiling until it was finished. Within a week, everything was back to normal.

That incident taught me something about human nature. Every kid gets into trouble. Every kid has the potential to do something disastrous. Every kid sooner or later disobeys his parents. Children also have the ability to lie and deceive themselves. The heart is deceptive, and such a defect does not disappear with age. It simply becomes more sly and cunning as we get older. "The heart is hopelessly dark and deceitful, a puzzle that no one can figure out" (Jeremiah 17:9 *The Message*). The only remedy for a fallen nature and a deceptive heart is to grab hold of God's heart.

This book embraces three important pillars that help us break barriers and attain a life of significant meaning and fulfillment. The first pillar represents a strong rejection of corruption, cheating, malice, hatred, fear, lying, and unfaithfulness. It is a move toward embracing the character and heart of God the Father.

This chapter helps us construct the pillar of God's heart in our lives. We'll examine our hearts in light of God's goodness and learn the steps necessary to create a godly heart.

Godly character is the most fundamental and important building block of our lives. Everything we do, think, and say reflects what is on the inside. For what we do is a reflection of who we are. We are not who we are because of what we do. We do what we do because of who we are. Everything honest, godly, virtuous, and decent comes from God's heart. If we want to establish the first pillar in our lives, we must embrace all these qualities and live them in everything we say and do.

## THE MIRROR NEVER LIES

During my first two years of college, I worked at a Sears Parts and Service Center in Santa Ana, California. There was one day each year I disliked intensely: inventory day. Counting every single screw, plastic part, and anything not nailed down filled the most painstaking eight hours I spent each January. Taking inventory was uncomfortable. It was time-consuming. At times, it was painful. But in spite of the nuisance it represented, I understood that it was necessary.

Taking inventory is like going to the doctor and having your cholesterol or blood pressure checked. Undoubtedly, the doctor tells you to exercise more, eat better, and reduce your stress levels. After the whole experience of being poked and prodded with instruments and needles, you think, *I felt fine before I walked in. So why do I feel so lousy after my checkup?* This is because the doctor has taken an inventory of your health and told you the truth about your condition. Yes, it is painful at times. Yes, it is time-consuming. Yes, it is uncomfortable and intimidating. But ultimately, it is necessary.

There comes a time in all our lives when we must face the facts. We must look in the mirror and accept the truth about who we are as spouses, parents, children, people, and children of God. The mirror never lies. We must accept the good and the bad. Only then can we begin to take the proper steps to bring our hearts into alignment with God's. This is essential because the heart is very deceitful: "A malicious man disguises himself with his lips, but in his heart he harbors deceit" (Proverbs 26:24 NIV).

Too many people are ignorant about the condition of their hearts. Many of us think things are better than they actually are. In many ways, it's like gaining weight. We don't realize how much

26

food we consume in a day, and at the end of the month, when we step onto the scale, we can't believe we've gained another couple of pounds. The same is true about debt. Many of us spend much more than we realize. But at the end of the month, reality stares at us from a computer screen, credit card statement, or checkbook. The same is true about the clutter hidden in our hearts. Much of the time, we are unaware of how much darkness lurks in our innermost being.

When you take a look at what's on the inside, what do you discover? What do you say when you are driving alone on the busy streets of your city? Do you break the laws of the road? What thoughts do you entertain when you are standing in line alone at the bank and no one recognizes who you are? How do you behave on your beach vacation? What questionable things do you do that you wouldn't do at home? How do you act around strangers? What TV shows do you watch when you can't sleep at night or when no one else is home? What do you say behind your colleague's back? Do you manage your finances ethically? What are the sins and dark patterns of destruction lurking within your heart?

The Bible says in Romans 3:23: "All have sinned and fall short of the glory of God" (NIV). This means regardless of how *good* we are, we're still guilty of something. Being *good* isn't good enough. No one is exempt. No one is perfect. For this reason, it is vital that we embrace God's mercy and forgiveness. God the Father offers us His very heart. Now is the time to take it!

## THE HEART OF THE MATTER

The heart of God the Father values and projects love, kindness, patience, holiness, virtue, righteousness, justice, truth, honesty, faithfulness, steadfastness, respect, discipline, integrity, service, teachability, and self-esteem. In the face of diversity, challenge, or daily routine, these traits govern our actions and responses. Throughout the remainder of this chapter, we will learn the five steps of creating the first pillar, the heart of the Father.

## 1. Desire to Create a Godly Heart

Everything we do is initiated by want. We must yearn for a godly heart. We must have a deep longing to take on God's character and values. Once we have decided a godly heart is imperative for our lives, we can begin the process of becoming all we are meant to be.

My quest for spiritual redemption began at fifteen years of age. I looked into the mirror the morning after another night of partying in my small hometown. I had spent the night at my friend's house after downing a six-pack of Schlitz Malt Liquor. I remember the beer vividly, especially its extraordinary buzz. Even worse, I remember its rancid smell on my clothes. I am not sure which is worse, the hangover or the smell of beer on your clothes. At that point, I was not an alcoholic. But the patterns of alcoholic destruction were rapidly forming in my adolescent life. I drank a couple of beers a week. To make things worse, my friend's parents spent a lot of time away from home, and as a result we were left unsupervised when we hung out.

As I stared into the mirror with bloodshot eyes and a bird's nest for hair, I said to myself and to God, *Oh, Lord, I don't want to become what I am becoming. God, please help me change! I want to leave this life of destruction.* At that moment the desire to change was birthed into my heart. I wasn't sure what I wanted to become, but I knew beyond a shadow of a doubt what I did not want to become. I knew I didn't want to become a drunkard or someone who let his life slip away into substance abuse. I wanted my life to count for something significant.

Don't discount the importance of this first step. A change of heart begins with desire. And not only will having the heart of God enable you to break your barriers, it will most definitely save you from making choices that will forever scar your life and your loved ones.

Still not convinced? Perhaps you're saying, "I know I need to work on being a better person. I know I should strive to have a godly heart, but I just don't see why this is so important. *Is it really that urgent?*"

Good question!

A friend told me about a beer party that was held in the home of a college senior named Sean. It was a small get-together with only three students. The two seniors, Jeremy and Sean, were a bit more adventurous and decided to smoke a bong and down a six-pack, while David, the freshman, just watched. About halfway through their adventure, Jeremy handed Sean a codeine pill and said, "Here, try this!" His friend looked somewhat hesitant. Sean knew he had crossed the line by drinking and smoking, but he hadn't gone so far that he couldn't turn back. Jeremy insisted, "Trust me. You're going to love this." Then he turned and hit the wall with his fist. "Check it out, dude. I don't feel a thing!" Sean, somewhat reluctant, decided to pop the pill and quickly discovered that painkillers mixed with beer did indeed kill pain.

When Jeremy left to use the restroom, Sean suddenly stopped smiling. His whole demeanor changed. He slowly walked over and stood in front of the full-length mirror. Soberly glaring at the reflection of his feet, he raised his head until he stared into his own eyes. His disappointment was obvious. "What in the world are you doing?" he asked himself. Pausing for a moment, he broke eye contact, looked at the floor, and raised his head again. "You go to church! You know God! You study the Bible in Sunday school!" Then he sighed, shook his head in disgust, and said, "I can't believe I'm doing this," seemingly unaware of David, who was sitting in the corner and watching. With that, Jeremy returned, and the party continued.

That day, Sean made a choice. He decided to reject the still, small voice of godly reason. He decided *not* to embrace the heart of God. He chose to do things his way. He allowed temptation to sweep him away. Years of going to church and reading his Bible were replaced with a lifestyle of parties and promiscuity. But there was no harm, no foul. After all, where's the urgency for change, right?

Years passed, and one day Sean was in a bar in the heart of the city. This time, there was no voice of reason challenging his prodigal son behavior. One of his friends spotted him from across the room, came up behind him, and grabbed his arm. "Hey, I just bought a brand-new sports car. You want to see what this baby can do? Here," he said, tossing him the keys. "Why don't you drive?" Sean smirked, raised his right eyebrow, and said, "You bet!"

He jumped into the driver's seat, and they headed down the highway. Within minutes they were traveling 120 miles per hour. Unfortunately, Sean's impaired motor skills couldn't handle the poorly lighted highway or the curve with a speed limit of 60 miles per hour. The vehicle flew off the road and slammed head-on into a tree. The passenger never made it to the hospital. Sean, who was thrown from the vehicle, had hardly any scratches. Instead, he lives with the scar of his friend's death to this day.

But perhaps you don't struggle with substance abuse. Maybe you struggle with sexual promiscuity or some sort of compulsive or addictive behavior. Whatever your issues and temptations, you need to take a good look in the mirror. Are there things that need to change? If so, don't miss this opportunity to come clean. Each time we reject that still, small voice of God's leading, it grows faint. And with time, we may become deaf to it. Now is the time to get rid of the things we know don't belong in our hearts and replace them with the goodness of God. A change of heart begins with desire. We have to want it bad enough!

Yes, it is that urgent, because our lives depend on it!

## 2. Discover the Attributes of God's Character

Any human effort to describe God and His attributes falls short. That is why we refer to the Bible as a guide. Galatians 5:22–23 states, "The fruit of the spirit is love, joy, peace, patience, kindness, goodness, faithfulness, gentleness and self-control. Against such things there is no law" (NIV). Those words illuminate the character of God, His very essence. Let's take a look at a few of these traits independently.

*Love is a word used throughout the entire Bible to describe God's character.* First Corinthians 13:4–8 describes love: "Love is patient, love is kind. It does not envy, it does not boast, it is not proud. It is not rude, it is not self-seeking, it is not easily angered, it keeps no record of wrongs. Love does not delight in evil but rejoices with the truth. It always protects, always trusts, always hopes, always perseveres. Love never fails" (NIV).

The Father's heart is filled with love toward people, the earth, and all creation. He demonstrated this love by sending His only Son to die for the salvation of humanity. If we are going to live out God's love, we too will become selfless, forgiving, hopeful, slow to anger, and never-failing. And we will display these characteristics of love to our friends, family members, and even enemies.

31

Of all the attributes of God, love is the greatest. It is the most important ingredient in building a heart like God's. His love for us has no limits. Our ability to overcome the barriers we face is enhanced because He lovingly offers us what we need to become all that He's destined us to be.

*Joy is another godly characteristic.* It is not sorrowful, distressed, depressed, or anxious. According to the dictionary, joy is a sensation of elevated pleasure of a spiritual kind. Unfortunately, many people do not have joy in their lives. They find themselves frustrated with not reaching their goals and expectations. Even when they admittedly have everything they need, they cannot sense any joy. There is some missing element, or their life is never good enough.

But God's joy overshadows the disappointments of our daily lives. It fills us with contentment based not on circumstances but on a solid fact: We are God's children, and no matter what we do or do not do, God's profound love for us never changes. Imagine living life filled with joy regardless of the challenges you face!

*Patience is a virtue that seems to be slowly eroding from our culture.* Twenty years ago, the term "road rage" was not part of our vocabulary. Today, you hear it on the six o'clock news and read about it in the newspapers. But lack of patience isn't exclusive to driving. It exists in virtually every facet of life. More parents than ever admit they wish they had more patience with their kids. I know. I am one of them. At the end of their lives, most parents wish they had spent more time with their children and had more patience raising them.

God's patience, on the other hand, endures forever. It doesn't run out because we spilled a glass of milk or stole something. Humanity continues to move forward because God has not run out of patience with us. God exercises His patience toward all of us. He is slow to anger. No matter how many times we fail, His tolerance of our failures endures. If we are to embrace a heart like God's, patience must be an integral part of our character.

*Goodness is central to the heart and character of God.* The phrase "God is good" is heard every day in countries throughout the world. And those who display goodness exhibit to a certain degree the character of God. When one country offers assistance to another by sending food or humanitarian or financial aid, this is a display of goodness. When one friend helps another or when a spouse makes a sacrificial effort to help the other, that is a wonderful display of goodness.

*Kindness is enacted by showing sympathy and compassion toward others.* It is the demonstration of a considerate and caring attitude.

Several years ago, my daughters went to a school where traditional family and religious values were taught. Those values were part of the philosophy of the institution. Most of the teachers came from a religious affiliation similar to our own. Yet many of the children attending the school did not display such values. When smaller kids would trip and fall, older kids would laugh and make fun of them. Bad language and offensive behavior could be seen in many grade levels among many students. At times, racial comments and intolerance of those who came from other countries were a problem. In many classrooms, there was great disorder and rambunctious behavior. Teachers found it difficult to keep the upper hand and maintain the order necessary in a learning environment. Eventually, we moved our girls to another school—an international school with no religious affiliation or denominational ties.

The second school's students were mild mannered and displayed a wonderful culture of kindness to one another. When smaller kids fell down on the playground, older ones helped them to their feet and checked to see if they were injured. Students worked together in study groups to accomplish assignments and master the material. The students showed a high level of kindness toward one another, especially in comparison to the previous school.

Showing kindness requires effort. Simply because we attend a church or belong to a religious organization doesn't necessarily mean that we automatically display this very important aspect of God's heart. Kindness is a godly trait we demonstrate to others regardless of whether they are older, younger, richer, poorer, or more or less popular than we are. The good news is that when we grow closer to God, His heart enables us to show sympathy and compassion to others.

*Faithfulness is the trait of sticking it out in good times and bad.* The divorce rate continues to climb in many countries around the world. Old friends are dropped for more popular and influential acquaintances from one day to the next. Many employees talk behind their employers' backs and have very little loyalty toward their companies.

The Bible describes God as abounding in love and faithfulness. Exodus 34:6 says: "He passed in front of Moses, proclaiming, 'The LORD, the LORD, the compassionate and gracious God, slow to anger, abounding in love and faithfulness'" (NIV). Psalm 117:2 says, "Great is his love toward us, and the faithfulness of the LORD endures forever. Praise the LORD" (NIV).

A good friend who is on the board of directors for one of the largest radio networks in the United States once told me, "Jason, half the battle in life is showing up. If you make a commitment, stick with it. Be faithful every day—even in the little things—and God will bless you for it."

*Gentleness is the quality of being mild and kind in nature.* It means having a gracious and honorable way about yourself. It is godly to treat others with dignity in a manner that is tender and calm. When I think about how God has treated my family over the years, one word comes to mind: *gentleness.*

In spite of my stubbornness and, at times, prideful attitude, His still, small voice has taught me and led me through the darkest of times and the greatest of victories. When I look at my children and those living around me, I am reminded of the need to treat them with a gentle attitude in the same way God has treated me. I am encouraged to see them as God sees them: people created in His image. My prayer is that I will display the heart of God the Father by being gentle, wise, and loving.

*Self-control is a fundamental part of a godly heart.* Self-control is the ability to withstand temptation and maintain stability during turbulent times. In a day and age when a vast majority of the population is overeating, overspending, and undersleeping, now more than ever we need to embrace a heart of self-control. God offers us the power of self-control.

When Christ was in the desert being tempted by Satan, He hadn't eaten in forty days. His body was weak. He was tired and most likely dehydrated. Later, at the end of His ministry, He was tempted to walk away from it all. There in the Garden of Gethsemane, he could have walked away from the responsibility of the Cross. But He didn't give in to Satan and He didn't walk away from the Cross. And God offers us, through Jesus' amazing example, a wonderful model of self-control under fire. This too is a trait we will take on as we work together with the Lord to build a godly heart.

Remember, a godly heart is the first building block for breaking barriers. Sure, the world has ways of overcoming obstacles, but the only lasting and effective way is God's way. And we have this wonderful assurance: when we ask God to create within us a heart like His, He is faithful to complete the work!

## 3. Ask God for Help

It is impossible for us to take on the heart of God and live out His attributes unless He helps us do so. God is more than willing to help us. We are His children. He loves us and desires to give us all that is necessary to break barriers. So then, what remains? What is the prerequisite to having a godly heart? We need to ask Him for help.

After discovering the attributes of God, we ask Him through prayer to help us make those attributes part of who we are. We need to ask two things of the Lord: to create in us a heart like His, and to show us through tangible examples how we can live out His characteristics.

My mom has suffered many difficult trials and has overcome many barriers. In 1991, she lost her second husband to a long bout with cancer. After more than ten years of marriage, she found herself a sudden widow, packing household trinkets accumulated over time. Within a few short weeks, she returned to her secluded home in the small mountain community of Big Bear Lake, California. Although her battle with depression and loneliness grew with each passing week, God never abandoned her. He kept watch over her.

One morning she decided she needed help to develop a heart like God's and to leave her disordered alcoholic life behind. She looked in the mirror and said a simple prayer to God: "Lord, help me set my life straight." Although she didn't list the attributes of God as I have done, in essence what she prayed for was a change of heart.

Within the year, many of the destructive patterns governing her life began to dissipate. Her addiction to alcohol was broken. She began to read the Bible, pray, and attend church on a regular basis. The qualities of God began to permeate her life. Soon thereafter, I noticed a radical change in her character. A woman who once struggled with a lack of patience, hurt, anger, fear, and depression began to display hope, faithfulness, love, holiness, and righteousness. Today, she is actively involved in her church, she helps seniors, and she volunteers at a soup kitchen during holidays.

How did all this start for her? It began with a simple prayer. She asked the Lord to help her put into practice godly traits, and the Lord responded. I am a witness to the revolutionary changes that have taken place in her life. Those who knew her before say she is a completely different person.

We too can call upon the Lord, knowing that He hears us. Remember, He is all-powerful, and He wants to help us break the chains that hold us back. When we realize the importance of creating a heart like God's within us, we can count on Him to move mountains to help us attain this wonderful goal. This is why John 16:24 says, "Until now you have not asked for anything in my name. Ask and you will receive, and your joy will be complete"

(NIV). Also, Matthew 7:7 says, "Ask and it will be given to you; seek and you will find; knock and the door will be opened to you"(NIV). God is eager to answer such a petition and grant us a godly heart. His desire is for us to become people full of goodness, holiness, righteousness, and virtue.

As we ask the Lord for a godly heart, it is important that we also request tangible examples to serve as a model for us. As a result of our prayers, the Lord will respond by providing clear examples of His attributes and by creating opportunities to put them into practice.

Consider the following prayer as a guide to ask the Lord to help you build a heart like His:

> *Lord, I want You to create in me a clean heart, one full of love, joy, and patience. You are full of virtue, and I desire to reflect Your wonderful character in this world. Help me to reflect Your goodness, kindness, and faithfulness. In those times when I am challenged to uphold Your principles, help me to be gentle and full of self-control. Most of all, help me to reflect Your love to a world that desperately needs connection with You. I ask You to place clear signposts in my life so I can see Your godly attributes in action. Help me to assimilate Your heart and all its characteristics into my life. I ask these things in Christ's name. Amen.*

## 4. Put Godly Qualities into Practice

Godly attributes won't become ours through osmosis. We must work at developing them. We must be diligent. We cannot just wait for things to happen. Instead, we need to act upon what we know is right and godly, even when we feel unprepared.

Several years ago, I read about an organization that holds a biannual national publicity summit in New York City. More than seventy producers from the major television networks as well as stations and cable networks around the country are invited. They also bring in representatives from many of the top radio stations and magazines to meet authors and entrepreneurs who are trying to get their books, products, or services into the media. Only one hundred authors and entrepreneurs are admitted into the program. This gives each attendee ample time to make a decent presentation to the thirty or forty producers of his or her choosing.

When I saw their Web site mentioning the enormous opportunity, I thought, *This could be the breakthrough I need to obtain greater publicity for my book.* Although I had the desire to become a published author and understood that publicity was vital to a book's success, like many, I struggled with feelings of uncertainty.

I remember the battle that went on in my mind trying to decide whether or not I should attend:

*Am I truly ready for this?*

*Is this the right time?*

*Will anyone get behind my book?*

*These are the big leagues. Do I really belong here? I believe I do, but I am not sure.*

Over and over in my mind, the desire for excellence clashed against the spirit of self-doubt. Finally, one night while I was jogging, the Lord placed a very strong impression upon my heart. *Do you plan on getting any younger?* "No" I replied. *Then what are you waiting for? Are you waiting until you turn forty-five? Will you be better prepared at fifty or sixty? Seriously, what are you waiting for?*

I had no answer. I had no excuse.

I realized that taking on the heart of God is doing what you know you ought to do even when you feel inadequate or intimidated. Developing the heart of God requires action. Unfortunately, many people feel they should wait until they have their acts together before they attempt something God wants them to do, including creating a godly heart.

So I put my uncertainty to one side and signed up. Because of the experience and training I received at the summit, doors in the media began to open, and the book found its way into the hands of one of the most prestigious publishers in the world. The book in your hands is the product of following the Lord's prompting and walking through an open door.

Sometimes we need to be encouraged, nudged, or flat-out hit over the head. Sometimes we need to stop thinking about what we should do and start doing it. Yes, becoming more like the Lord is hard work, but you will never get there by contemplation alone. Don't let life happen to you. Don't let it pass you by. Aim for a godly heart by putting into action what you know are the qualities of His heart.

So if you have the desire for the heart of God, the knowledge about what it is, and God's help to go after it, what are you waiting for? You've asked the Lord for help, and He will respond. Don't just sit there feeling unworthy or wondering if God will reject you. You are destined for greatness. God has opened a door for you and has a great purpose for your life. You are by no means an accident. The Lord has planned for this moment since the beginning of time. So seize the opportunity. Go for it. You will not regret it.

Because this is so important, I want to summarize the process before we move on. We assimilate the character of God into our own hearts by acting out these traits in our lives. We aggressively look for opportunities to love, be kind, and express patience to others. As we love others, we become loving people. When we are kind to others, we become kind people. When we express patience toward others, we become patient people. Wherever the head leads, the heart will follow. Therefore, decide to love. Decide to be kind. Decide to be patient. Decide to be holy, virtuous, forgiving, and full of joy. Act out your decisions. You will notice these traits becoming part of who you are. The transformation does not happen overnight. But as we act out these habits, it will bring about a transformation in our hearts. Eventually, we become those things we long to become.

I have purposely not included a section in this book on how to avoid ungodliness. Christians have a tendency to define godliness as avoiding evil: "Don't do this! Don't do that!" This is an unhealthy approach to trying to be godly. Instead, we should pursue the attributes of God so energetically that we do not have time for or interest in ungodly things. One of the best ways to make sure we pursue godly attributes instead of carnal ones is to surround ourselves with godly people. This brings us to the fifth step.

## 5. Form a Small Accountability Group

It is best to form an accountability group with people who understand godliness and who care about becoming godly people themselves. If you pick friends who have little regard for godliness, they probably will not serve you well in an accountability group. Surround yourself with people who pull you up to the next level instead of tearing you down. Pick three or four close friends who have godly standards and who care about your well-being. Sit down and explain what you want to accomplish. Make a list of the attributes you desire and how you can take practical steps to reach them. Ask your close friends to watch your progress as you pursue these qualities in everyday life. When in doubt, tell them about your dilemmas and challenges and ask them for help. Be sounding boards for one another in your quests for godliness.

When commercial pilots fly from one city to another, they have a full panel of instruments that keep track of the plane's altitude, longitude, airspeed, ground speed, mach speed, pitch, tail wind, head wind, and outside temperature. Some planes are equipped with satellite communications that inform the crew of their exact position in relation to the ground and topography. Such systems provide the crew with a down-to-the-minute estimation of their arrival time at their destination. Further, control towers along the entire route guide them and help them adjust their courses hundreds of miles before midair collisions could possibly occur.

With all the tools pilots have at their disposal in addition to the sophistication of modern aircraft, it's no wonder flying is the safest way to travel. These tools act as a virtual accountability group that helps pilots accomplish their task, getting people from one place to another safely, comfortably, and in a timely manner.

Just as pilots use instruments and control tower personnel to help them fly their planes, we too can look outside ourselves to accurately monitor our progress in creating a godly heart. Godly friends help us in our growth, guide us in our direction, and provide us with valuable perspective in times of difficulty and confusion.

You will see from your friends' feedback that becoming a godly person is much more attainable than you previously thought. After all, God wants this for you. No one wants you to grow and develop more than God. He is your biggest fan and your greatest admirer. He loves you and has great plans for your life.

According to Deuteronomy 28:1–14, God wants to bless you with great abundance; He wants to turn things around in your life. He wants to pour overwhelming provision into every area of your life and tip the scales in your favor. He wants to open great doors of opportunity and lavish you with good things. He wants to bless your children, grandchildren, and great grandchildren. He wants to give you many wonderful years of a blessed life. I am convinced that no matter what obstacle or barrier you are facing, with God, you will break it!

## FINDING TREASURE IN A TENT

All of the wonderful qualities mentioned earlier in this chapter come from God. They are His attributes. If we desire to be like Him and embrace His heart, these qualities must be part of who we are.

In March 2003, I was facing one of the biggest financial crises of my ministry. I had several financial commitments from churches in the United States that for various reasons were unable to fulfill their pledges for crusade sponsorship. As a result, I headed into the final weeks before a crusade on the verge of bankruptcy.

I started writing faxes and sending letters and e-mails asking for additional support. The response was minimal. Pastors were on vacation or out of the office. Individual donors were busy with business meetings. No matter what I did, no one seemed to be in a position to help. I came to an agonizing conclusion: my ministry was facing a debt of more than fifty thousand dollars. I would have to cancel a crusade and shut down our offices.

I remember the morning vividly. My wife and I headed out for a cup of coffee. Stopped at a stoplight and pondering the oncoming financial ruin, I broke down and wept. I cried like a baby. Normally I do not react that way, but my wife and I were alone, and it was a safe place to let it all out. I said to her, "I can't believe it's over. I can't believe after eleven years of building and planning, it has come to this disastrous finale."

As we sat down in the small café located in the heart of San José, we discussed the numbers and came to a conclusion. She said to me, "By Friday, March 31, we need five thousand dollars to pay the bills." I said, "All right. We'll ask the Lord for help. If we don't receive five thousand dollars, then I will let our staff go, close the offices, and cancel the upcoming crusade." This was one of the most painful decisions I have ever made.

Several days passed. On March 28, I received a call from a missionary who had just landed in Miami after his trip to Chile. Mike Shields is a good friend who loves the Lord deeply. His usual excited and highly enthusiastic voice filled the line as he said, "Jason! This is Mike! How ya doing, man?! Boy, I had an incredible trip. It was fantastic! Oh, thank You, Jesus! I just gave away forty thousand dollars to buy property for new churches. Isn't God great! Hey, as soon as I got off the plane, the Lord told me I had to send you five thousand dollars. So how do you want me to send it?"

My response was mixed with a bit of stuttering and the overwhelming sensation of *I must be dreaming*. I said, "You can send it to us Federal Express!"

Let me make something very clear to you. Missionaries are on tight budgets—they do not give money away just to give it away. So when a missionary senses the Lord is urging him to help out another missionary financially and he actually goes through with it by giving the money, God obviously orchestrated his actions.

Mike Shields sent us a miracle offering that met our deadline and helped us move one step closer to our goal. And he did it by displaying several of the characteristics of God. He reacted to a need with love, patience, joy, and kindness. He never said, "How could you let this happen?" Mike demonstrated the heart of God to us and to everyone in attendance at the crusade.

My wife, Cindee, and I were grateful to the Lord for His provision, but the experience left us with a different taste in our mouths. It seemed as though we had come too close to the flames of trial and felt a bit singed along the edges.

We started the crusade on a Tuesday night with both of our big tents set up. Our smaller tent measures approximately 15,000 square feet. The big one measures 35,000 square feet and holds close to 5,000 people. There was great excitement in the air, especially among our team members. They had experienced a financial miracle and were fired up about reaching a community that desperately needed to hear the message of hope.

On the other hand, I was somewhat disconnected. Still feeling sore from the spiritual battle two weeks before, I had a difficult time focusing. Perhaps I was being a baby or simply having difficulty swallowing the fact that we had come so close to a disaster. Although I was struggling, I was aware the Lord had His criteria and objectives.

I remember a man who came to the event and sat about thirty rows back. He looked awful, as if he had been run over by a truck. Toward the end of my message, I gave an invitation to those who wanted to start a relationship with Christ. He, along with several hundred others, came forward, asking God for forgiveness and for a godly heart. The next thing I knew, he had collapsed and was making weird sounds at the foot of the stage. The ushers picked him up and escorted him to the smaller tent adjacent to our big tent.

After a few minutes he recovered, and several counselors began to find out more about his life. The next night he came again, sat about thirty rows back, and came forward during the invitation at the end of the message. Once again, he passed out and the ushers took him to the other tent. This happened several nights until the final night. At the start of the Saturday night meeting, he sat in the back and listened to the music and the message. When I gave the last invitation for the crusade, he responded by coming forward. This time was different. This time he stayed in his right mind. This time would be unlike the others.

At the very end of the service, just before we dismissed the crowd, he motioned to me. I walked over to the edge of the stage, and my crusade coordinator said, "This gentleman wants to testify about the change in his life." I thought, *Well, it's the last night. What harm can there be in letting him have the microphone for a couple of minutes?*

He walked onto the stage nicely dressed and nodded as I handed him one of the stage microphones used by the singers. He turned to face the crowd of six thousand-plus people gathered there, and began to tell his story:

About eighteen months ago, my wife left me for another man. She took the kids and left me with nothing. Within the same time period, I lost my job as one of the top insurance salesmen in the country. I fell into a deep depression with no end in sight. I looked for ways to commit suicide. I tried combining liquor with sleeping pills, but nothing worked.

Then I remembered the highway leading toward the town of Limon. There is a bridge located about three miles from downtown San José. The bridge is located next to the Saprissa soccer stadium. The fall is close to five hundred feet. Everyone who has ever thrown himself or herself off the bridge has died. It seemed the only sure way to go. Last week, I decided to throw myself off the bridge and commit suicide.

I got up this past Tuesday morning with the intention of driving to the bridge and jumping Tuesday night. As I was driving down the road heading out of Guadalupe, I looked off to the left-hand side of the road and saw two big white tents with a sign that read "There Is Hope in Jesus." Those words penetrated my heart. I pulled off the road and pondered for a brief few moments. I thought, *Well, if there is no hope for me here, then I can always continue on to my date with destiny.*

I turned off my car, came in, and sat in the back. After the message, Jason gave an invitation to begin a relationship with Christ. So I went forward. The next thing I can remember is, I woke up in another tent. I thought this was weird. But every time I woke up night after night, I was surrounded by counselors who helped me discover the source of my pain and hurt.

They asked questions that helped pinpoint the very issues keeping me behind the barriers of self-destruction. They helped me overcome those diabolical voices of suicide that have been haunting me for the past eighteen months. They helped me find those in my past who had hurt me and those I needed to forgive. They helped me find the source of my pain. I can say for the first time in a year and a half that those voices have come to a grinding halt. Jesus has set me free, and He has broken the barriers in my life.

I don't know who I need to thank for putting up these two big white tents, but I've found a great treasure here. Whoever you are, thank you. And God bless you all.

He turned and gave me a heartfelt hug. The crowd cheered. Then he gave me the microphone and walked off the stage. I was speechless. My mind raced back to the week leading up to the thirty-first of March. I retraced my steps. Just like the famous poem "Footprints in the Sand," I could see only one set of prints, the Lord's. He carried us through the fire. He provided because He had a date with thousands of people and one very special individual.

Nine months later I asked the man to come back into our offices and videotape his testimony, which he kindly agreed to do. For the entire year following the crusade, he reported to us that he had no suicidal thoughts or depression. Since then, he has started a new job and with God's help has been highly successful in putting his life back together. He has displayed many of God's attributes such as self-control, goodness, faithfulness, gentleness, kindness, and, most important, peace.

As he faced the diabolical voices of suicide and torture, he managed to take the hand of God and rewrite the habits of his life. He's no longer bound by anxiety, suicidal thoughts, and self-hatred. He, like Mike Shields, is a wonderful example of someone who has grabbed hold of the heart of God the Father and broken the barriers separating him from becoming all he is destined by God to be. The man reached out in the most desperate moment of his life, and God responded.

God has all power, and His love for us is immeasurable. Our ability to break barriers comes when we become His children and reach for the gifts He's so happy to give us. Regardless of whether the barrier you face is modest or you feel like you're on your way to a bridge, you too can experience God's love. You can experience His power. God is more than willing to give you the necessary gifts to break the barriers that hold you back as you reach out to Him as your heavenly Father.

In this chapter, we've taken an in-depth look at the first pillar. We've looked in the mirror and examined our hearts in light of God's goodness. We've taken an inventory and discovered that every human being is born with a defect. This defect causes us to live for ourselves and covet unhealthy things. Without God, our moral development would be skewed and flawed. Now, more than ever, we need to create a godly heart—one that guides us to become all God destined us to be. Why is this important? Everything we do and say is a direct result of what is in our heart. Jesus said in Matthew 15:18, "The things that come out of the mouth come from the heart, and these make a man 'unclean'" (NIV). The first step toward breaking the barriers is to develop a godly heart. Remember the five steps to acquiring God's heart:

1. Desire to create a godly heart.
2. Discover the attributes of God's character.
3. Ask God for help.
4. Put godly qualities into practice.
5. Form a small accountability group.

In the next chapter, we'll continue our discussion of the first pillar. This is where you'll discover God's mission for your life. It promises to be one of the most powerful tools for our journey.

As we close this chapter together, let me share a prayer with you that may help you work to create a godly heart. Aside from the desire, the most important element is God's help. Without God, it is impossible to set a course for breaking barriers. As you begin your day, follow this prayer and meditate on it throughout the day. I have taken a portion of it from Psalm 51:9–12 NIV.

> *Dear Lord, I recognize I need Your help. I have made many mistakes and have failed many times in my life. I recognize I need a godly heart, one like Yours. "Hide your face from my sins and blot out all my iniquity. Create in me a pure heart, O God, and renew a steadfast spirit within me. Do not cast me from your presence or take your Holy Spirit from me. Restore to me the joy of your salvation and grant me a willing spirit, to sustain me." I give You my heart and ask You to mold it, change it, and make it new. I accept You as my Lord and Savior and ask You to sit on the throne of my life. May Your love, joy, patience, kindness, goodness, faithfulness, gentleness, and self-control permeate my life for the rest of my days. I turn my life over to You. Do with it as You will. I ask these things in Christ's name. Amen.*

CHAPTER 3

# Unleashing the Power of God's Heart
# in Your Life

BIRTHDAYS are always a highlight of the year for kids. In October 2002, my wife and girls, missionary associate Ashley Rutledge, and myself were planning to celebrate my oldest daughter's birthday by playing laser tag at the mall. The girls got up as excited as ever, ready to see who could get the highest score. But we all knew what their goal was: dethroning Dad as the top scorer.

In Central America, October is the rainiest month of the season. However, this Saturday morning met us with a surprise welcome of sunshine and clear skies. We headed to the Mall San Pedro, located across the street from the University of Costa Rica. It is the central mall of the city and the closest shopping center to downtown San José. It has become a cultural center for movies, entertainment, and shopping.

Upon our arrival we found an ideal parking spot and immediately headed toward the food court for lunch. The mall was fairly full for the noon hour, and the people in front of us were walking slowly. As I looked for an opportunity to pass the slow herd migrating toward the watering hole, I noticed a young man walking near the front of the pack.

Although I didn't have a clear view of him, I could see he was wearing a black shirt. Strolling through the mall with no purpose whatsoever, he seemed to be listening to a CD. The back of his black shirt was unclear at first. I managed to catch the first word, which was written in white letters. It said "Jesus." I recognized it as an English shirt and not Spanish, because "Jesus" did not have an accent mark over the "u." As a crusade evangelist, it intrigued me to see a shirt making a public proclamation in English in a Hispanic culture. I tried to get a better view by craning my neck to see over the heads of those walking in front of us.

All of a sudden, I managed to catch a glimpse of the second word just beneath the first. It said "is." *Umm, Jesus is,* I thought. *What could the rest of his shirt say?* From a distance, I could gather there were four words in all, but I was unable to decipher the remaining two. By now, as you can imagine, curiosity was eating me alive. Still, there were about twenty people separating us. Little by little they shifted in different directions, and after about ten seconds, I was able to view the third word. It was the word "a."

The phrase "Jesus is a" can have a wide variety of endings. The prospects are endless. As someone serving in ministry, I was excited to see someone make a public statement about the answer every society needs to hear. Unable to pass the traffic in front of me, I exercised patience and waited a few more seconds. Finally the waters parted. The people in front of me moved to either side. There he was, without any visual interference. Nothing separated us, and I could see his shirt entirely. The last word, however, was not what I had expected. Better stated, it was the antithesis of my expectations.

It was one of the worst vulgarities you can imagine. Associated with the female anatomy, the word is hardly used in R-rated movies because of its overwhelming graphic implication. At first, I thought I was misreading it. I looked for a possible wrinkle covering up a couple of extra letters. But there was no such luck. My eyes were not failing me.

I turned to my wife in utter shock and said, "Honey, do your eyes see what my eyes see on the back of that guy's shirt?" Her response said it all. Although she never uttered a word, her reply summed up everything I felt. Making a gasping sound, she sucked in three gallons of air and raised her eyebrows to the top of her forehead as if someone had thrown near-freezing water all over her back. The answer was yes. My eyes were telling me the truth.

Ashley's response was the same as my wife's. The three of us continued for a few seconds without saying a word. The girls, thank the Lord, didn't see anything. They probably wouldn't have understood it if they had, which is a blessing as well.

Within each of us lives a Pharisee, a part of us that is very legalistic. He may be small, medium, or large, but he exists. In circumstances such as this, he pops his ugly little head up and makes himself known. For this reason, the first words out of our mouths were, "Where is security? This guy needs to be removed from the premises." I understand there are liberties when it comes to freedom of speech. But this sort of thing went way beyond one's right to freedom of expression. In a mall full of families and children, such vulgarity and blasphemy were completely uncalled for, regardless of free speech rights.

The young man reached the food court and continued on at his very slow pace. I realized at this point he was not there to shop but to show. He became a walking billboard for the worst advertisement I had ever seen. His sole purpose was to display his shirt as he strolled through the mall. He rounded a corner and made his way in the opposite direction from which we had arrived at the food court.

I turned to my wife and said, "Well, I don't see security any-where. Honey, you need to pray for me." "Why?" she asked. "Be-cause I'm going after him!" And that's exactly what I did. It took me about fifteen seconds to catch up to him, partially because he was cruising at a snail's pace.

I tapped him on the shoulder, and he immediately spun around. He had an expression on his face that suggested he had been wait-ing for someone to respond to the blasphemous declaration. "Fi-nally, a customer," was the look he gave me. When I saw the front of his shirt, I discovered it was worse than the back. It had a full frontal nudity photo of a nun. She was obviously a young model. Over the top of her head were the words "Parable of Filth" in bloodred Gothic writing.

Then I heard the voice of the Lord speak to me, saying, *Do it in love, Jason. Do it in love.* The young man was staring at me, waiting on my reason for interrupting his Saturday afternoon stroll. Suddenly, in the awkward moment of silence, I began to grin. Within several seconds my grin turned into laughter. I thought, *Lord, here I am in front of someone with a horrific shirt and with nothing to say.*

At times we need a mission, one based on godly character and guided by godly principles. We need a mission led by godly love and conviction. As it seemed at the time, I had conviction but no mission. So I did the only thing I could think of. I asked the Lord to give me the words. I asked Him to give me the right mission. I remembered Luke 12:11–12: "When you are brought before synagogues, rulers and authorities, do not worry about how you will defend yourselves or what you will say, for the Holy Spirit will teach you at that time what you should say" (NIV).

I grabbed hold of that Scripture and prayed, *Lord, help me. I don't know what to say.* I found myself with strong convictions to say and do something, but the words were absent. Then something shot out of my mouth. As I continued to chuckle I said, "You know, I have talked to rich people, poor people, happy people, sad people, short people, tall people, people who were demon-possessed, and people who were in their right minds. I've talked with married people, divorced people, people in North America, South America, young people, and old people. But in all my travels, I have never seen a shirt like that."

He responded forcefully, "Are you saying I am demon-possessed?!"

I did not respond verbally, but inwardly I thought, *Um, could be.*

The first question I asked him was if he spoke English. It was possible he was wearing a shirt he did not understand. Most articles of clothing that come to Latin America from the United States, for example, can be worn without question. If people receive a new shirt but do not understand what it says, they will most likely put it on anyway. Often, I see pastors attending ministers' retreats in Central America wearing light beer paraphernalia, although many do not know what "Budweiser" is. One year, I saw a pastor wearing a "Bud Light" deliveryman's overall. It probably came to Central America through the Salvation Army. Nonetheless, he was happily covered from head to toe by his new friends at Anheuser-Busch.

When I asked this young man if he spoke English, he said he didn't. Breathing a sigh of relief, I asked him if he understood what his shirt said. He responded, "Oh, yes. I had it translated."

Instead of conjuring up a debate on whether or not he was outside the boundaries of freedom of speech, I said, "Tell me, what kind of hurt or pain have you endured that has caused you to cry out in such anger at God?"

He replied, "I don't hate God. I have a relationship with God."

I said, "Well, demons have a relationship with God, but not the kind of relationship you or I would like to have."

Soon, a small group of people had accumulated around us, and I began to share with the fellow: "Let's assume after a morning meal of black beans and rice, the skin of one black bean gets stuck to your top front teeth. Every time you open your mouth, all anyone can see is a big black slimy bean covering your smile. On your way to work, people on the bus don't say anything. People at your job see it but do not say anything either. Your acquaintances in the lunchroom don't say anything. Every time you open your mouth all people see is a big black bean. Would you feel comfortable going through the day without anyone helping you? Or would you want someone to tell you about the ugly smelly stain ruining your smile?" The crowd continued to grow, totaling about ten.

The Lord could not have given me a better analogy, although I did not think about it at the time. Costa Ricans are practically religious when it comes to oral hygiene. Many of them take their toothbrushes with them to school and work to brush between meals. I had forgotten how sensitive they are about the subject, but the Lord had not forgotten. He used a cultural inroad to speak to a confused and hurt young man. When I asked whether he would want help in that embarrassing situation, he looked down and said, "Yes. I would want someone to tell me about that."

Then I said, "Well, the shirt you are wearing is a thousand

times worse than a black bean stuck to your tooth. You are wearing a walking billboard proclaiming a message you do not intend to say. I assume you do not hate God. But the meaning of this shirt communicates to all of us you are deeply disturbed, troubled, hurt, and have a tremendous amount of hatred toward Him.

"I might venture to say that when you lie down at night and when all noise is silenced in your house, you begin to experience haunting, diabolic voices in your head that rob you of all peace. You stare at the ceiling, wishing the night would last forever so as not to face another day. No matter what you do, you cannot silence those voices. So you try to drown them out with drugs, music, and alcohol, but nothing works. I might dare to say you have looked for meaning, significance, joy, peace, and love. Unfortunately, all you have found is greater isolation and longer shadows. I think it is somewhat ironic you are mocking Someone who happens to be your only solution.

"The Someone to whom I am referring can set you free and deliver you from your incarceration. He can break the chains of darkness that have you bound in despair. His name is Jesus, and He died for you on the cross of Calvary. He is the King of kings and Lord of lords. He is the key to open the door of your life, and He would like to help you."

Tears welled up in his eyes as he gazed at the floor. Several people were still standing around listening to the conversation. Then I extended my hand to him, asking if I might have the privilege of praying for him. He said, "You know, I would like to see change in my life, but it has to be a desire from my heart. Something within me has to want it more than anything, but I am not ready."

"That's all right," I said. "One day you will be, and I will continue to pray for you until you are."

Afterward, I gave him a piece of paper containing our Web site address, e-mail, and post office information. Then I told him to contact me anytime he needed help. He shook my hand in gratitude and turned and walked away. The small crowd around us began to disburse as well, and I turned and headed back to join my wife and girls for the birthday celebration.

I had a mission. At the time, I wasn't sure how to fulfill it. But I knew I needed to do something. My convictions told me that. I didn't know what to do at the time. Nonetheless, my mission was a godly one. No matter what circumstances I might find myself in, God will help me plot a godly course that is significant and meaningful. A course that is meaningful not only for *my* life but for the lives of those with whom I come in contact. This mission helps me break the barriers and attain the great destiny God intends for me.

In this chapter, we continue our focus on the first pillar by taking what we've learned in the previous chapters to form a godly mission statement for our life. I like to call it "the golden thread." It's what you were created to be, why you're here, and what you'll be remembered for. It's your God-given call and reason for being. It's the one thing that makes you completely unique. When opposition rises against you, when the barriers seem impassable, when there seems to be no solution in sight, God's mission for your life serves as an anchor. That's your golden thread.

A well-defined mission doesn't change. A godly mission statement goes with you regardless of your career, educational level, or marital status. As you endeavor to break the barriers, it will give you great clarity and help you navigate through the most difficult challenges. It promises to be one of the most powerful tools for our journey.

A clearly defined mission is a gift from God, and He wants you to have this gift. How do you define your mission? I began in 1985 after finishing my first semester of college. I put down on paper how I wanted people to remember me after I died. I wrote down my legacy before I lived it. Priorities, values, qualities, and godly traits became the central focal point in defining who I was in my mission statement. Twenty years later, a large part of this original mission statement still guides me. It is well defined and lived. Now, what about you?

## WRITING YOUR FUTURE

Imagine for a moment you are going to a funeral. No one is ever enthusiastic about burying someone, especially a loved one. After you wake up and shower, you find some black attire and head to the church. Unfortunately, there is a lot of traffic on the road, and as a result, you arrive several minutes late. There is something different about this funeral, however: before the ceremony can begin, everyone in attendance must view the body.

As you pull into the driveway, you notice the parking lot is full and everyone is inside. You approach the front door and realize there is no music playing, nor is anyone speaking. Everyone is silently waiting for the final person to arrive. Walking down the center aisle, you turn to your right and left where everyone is sitting in place, waiting for the commencement. Your spouse and children have already arrived. All your friends are there. All your close relatives are there. Your most cherished loved ones are present. Everyone who has played a significant and meaningful role in your life over the years is in attendance. All of a sudden, you discover someone you did not expect to be there. God has made a cameo appearance and is seated in the front row as well.

At the front of the church is an open casket surrounded by candles and beautiful floral arrangements. The person inside the open coffin is dressed elegantly. The attention to detail is impeccable. Not one hair is out of place. To your surprise, however, it is not the person you expected. Instead, you discover it's you. No, this is not a horror flick. Yes, you are attending your own funeral, and now you are about to hear what your loved ones, your most cherished friends, and God will say about you.

You take a seat in the front row next to the Lord. He winks at you and gives you a squeeze just behind the kneecap. Then the ceremony begins. After hearing one of your favorite songs sung by an outstanding vocalist, the minister says, "Instead of hearing a sermon from me about our dearly departed, we are going to hear from those who mattered most to the deceased."

One by one, your children, spouse, parents, relatives, friends, coworkers, and God stand behind the podium and share the impact you made on their lives. They share what you meant to them. They share about your love, kindness, and goodness. Instead of hearing about all the money you made or about the property you purchased, you hear words of meaning and significance. They use you as an example of what it means to have good personal character. The words they use are not bound by time or space. They are terms and qualities that last forever.

Ask yourself the following questions (popularized in Stephen Covey's best seller *The Seven Habits of Highly Effective People*):

- What would you like to be said about you at your funeral?
- What do you want your spouse to say about you?
- What do you want your children and closest friends to say?
- What would you like God to say?

Think about some of the comments you would like your family and friends to make at your funeral. As you begin, try to incorporate the attributes of God outlined in the previous chapter into the comments you'd like to have spoken at your funeral. If we are going to break the barriers and become all God destined us to be, we must build a godly heart and a godly mission. It is vital to integrate the characteristics of the heart of God the Father into what we desire to become.

On separate sheets of paper, write out what you would like each of the following people to say about you when you depart from this life: spouse, children, family, close friends, parents, coworkers, and God. Take your time in contemplating what you would like them to say. This is one of the most important steps in forming a godly mission.

This exercise is not about what you think your loved ones might say today but what you want them to say at the end of your life. For example, you might write: "I would like my children to say I was a loving and patient father who took the time to listen to their concerns. I nurtured them and believed in them, creating in them a healthy self-esteem." And they might say, "Dad was a man who loved the Lord and displayed Christ's love to all of us and especially to those who were less fortunate."

Believe it or not, the attributes you list are the essence of your aspirations. They describe your golden thread. They represent the core values of the legacy you wish to leave behind. I call it the crystal ball effect. It's your history written in advance. You have just written down how you want people to remember you. When all the dust settles in your life, when there is nothing left but who you are and all has been stripped away, these words you've written will be the primary way people remember you. When all sickness ceases, when riches fade away and fame becomes a distant memory, the things mentioned above are the qualities you want people to be reminded of when your name is mentioned. A friend of mine once said, "I cannot be blamed for the name my parents gave me. But I can be blamed for what people think when they hear my name mentioned."

As you combine the godly attributes discussed in the previous chapter with what you want your loved ones to say about you, you begin to form a mission statement with purpose, significance, meaning, and most important: godliness. Once you form a mission statement based upon the attributes of the heart of God, the first pillar will be firmly established in your life. This gives you a clear purpose and a strong sense of direction. Here's how to do it.

## FORMING A GODLY MISSION

Summarize your life in one sentence. Try not to attach titles such as salesman or housewife to your mission statement. Concentrate on the one profound legacy you wish to leave behind in the minds of your loved ones. Find your *golden thread*. What and who you are is much more important than what you do. Remember, we do what we do because of who we are. We are not who we are because of what we do. So write down who you are in one honest but simple sentence, an uncomplicated description of who you are. Follow this sentence with individual statements (supporting points) that provide clarity to specific areas of your life.

I discovered a great passage of Scripture that defines who Jesus is. Luke recorded in the book of Acts a message preached by Peter, in which Jesus is not described as a man who preached to thousands or built a huge empire. Peter doesn't speak about material wealth, countries conquered, or fame. Instead, this passage is a mission statement about the greatness of the person of Christ. It talks about what He came to accomplish, how He impacted those around Him, and how people's lives were changed as a result of their contact with Him. It features a handful of powerful qualities and accomplishments pertaining to His life, leaving out only His crucifixion and resurrection.

> *God anointed Jesus of Nazareth with the Holy Spirit and with power. Then Jesus went around doing good and healing all who were oppressed by the devil, for God was with him.* (Acts 10:38 NLT)

First, this verse says Jesus of Nazareth was anointed by God with the Holy Spirit and with power. He was a man who came from a humble town and was filled with God's Spirit. It is implicit that He had the heart of God the Father. The conviction and power of God backed His ministry with the outward evidence of signs and wonders. Jesus was a man from Nazareth, and He was holy, righteous, and backed 100 percent by God.

Next, it says he went around doing good. What a great compliment Peter pays Jesus with these words. Very few times in my life have I ever heard someone give another person such praise. "Went around doing good" is one of the greatest accomplishments of anyone in the human race.

But Peter doesn't stop there. He continues by saying, ". . . and healing all who were oppressed by the devil." This summarizes Christ's ministry in just a few simple words. Not only was Jesus holy, anointed by the Holy Spirit, and backed by God, but also He went around doing good. He also went way beyond what is required of any human being by going into the devil's territory and freeing those who had been incarcerated by Satan. This implies

He had a physical healing ministry as well as a spiritual one. He reached into people's bodies, souls, and spirits and set them free. Notice Peter doesn't refer to Christ as one who discriminates against anyone based on age, gender, or race. Peter uses the word *all*. *Everyone* with whom Jesus came in contact experienced complete healing. All were candidates and recipients of Christ's healing power, setting them free from the clutches of the devil.

Finally, Peter closes his description of Jesus by stating that all this was accomplished because "God was with Him." What would direct Christ to lead such an outstanding and self-sacrificing life? Obviously, love is the first thing that comes to our minds. But there is something more there than love. Christ lived such a life because God was with Him. Christ had the heart of God the Father. He had a godly mission, and God stood with Him.

This verse not only expresses an admiration of the godly heart and mission Jesus had on earth, but in this closing element of the mission statement of Christ, once again, Peter recognizes God's backing and full support of Jesus' ministry.

When I study this passage of Scripture, I feel challenged to live an outstanding life. After I die, I want people to say God was with me. I desire to be remembered as a man who went around doing good and shared God's healing with those who were under the power of the devil. I want people to say I was full of the Holy Spirit and power.

Obviously, you do not have to cut and paste Christ's mission statement into yours, but it is helpful to see the legacy He left behind and how this affected Peter profoundly. As you construct your mission statement, model the structure of Peter's description of Christ, using several supporting points to give greater clarity to your general mission statement. Your mission statement can include subcategories (supporting points) or bullets embracing marriage, work, parenting, and spiritual and physical health. Or you can make individual mission statements for each of those areas.

Regardless of what format you choose, put together a statement that works for you. Remember, you should create something that can be understood by those around you and reflects the qualities and godly attributes we have outlined in this book so far.

In order to be lasting and effective, your mission statement must be based on the character of God. It must be congruent with God's direction and will for your life. Your mission statement isn't exclusively about you. It isn't exclusively about Him. It is a charge that reflects your partnership with Him to complete the mission He has placed on your life.

Use a separate piece of paper to sketch out your mission statement and how you want to be remembered.

## KEEP YOUR EYES FOCUSED ON THE GOAL

Paul Finkenbinder is an evangelist known throughout all Latin America. He has a four-minute program transmitted via television and radio, and the transcripts are printed in newspapers in every country. Few modern-day communicators of God's message of salvation have had the impact he has had. A few years back, we were having breakfast together. I asked him to give me in a nutshell the essentials for forming a ministry that would have an international impact for decades to come. He smiled and pulled out a piece of paper and jotted down his thoughts. (You can find more information about his ministry at www.box100.org.)

The first point was, "Find your lifetime goal." This is, in fact, where most of the world has failed. Most people have no idea where they are going. But today, you have taken a proactive step and done something that will change your life forever. Writing down your mission statement sets you apart from the millions of people who are helplessly floundering through life. Finding your lifetime goal and building it upon the foundation of a godly heart firmly establishes the first pillar as you endeavor to break barriers. A godly mission points you in the right direction and equips you with the first tool for becoming all you were destined to be.

In my conversation with Paul Finkenbinder, he touched on a second point: "Judge all choices against that goal." This means you must constantly evaluate your direction and decisions in light of the lifetime goal you have outlined for yourself. When temptations come, when distractions arise, when diversions interrupt, weigh all your options against the golden thread of what you desire to become. When an innovative opportunity presents itself, when a door is unlocked and springs open, when a new possibility comes your way or when a fresh prospect is discovered, practice caution by considering whether or not it will help you attain your lifetime goal.

Many ideas sound good at first. Many opportunities look favorable at the onset. Few serve to advance you toward your goal, however. On the other hand, some derailments can be blessings in disguise. Some interruptions or deviations are exactly what you need to become all you are destined to be. Therefore, you must carefully examine every opportunity that comes your way.

## YOUR BOAT WILL NEVER SINK

One day, the disciples learned an important lesson in not wavering from the vision God had placed in their hearts. Many of them were experienced fishermen. They navigated through some of the most difficult storms. They had seen almost every kind of wind condition and ocean current.

Luke 8:22–25 tells us a fascinating story. After a long day's work, Jesus turned to his disciples and said, "Let's cross to the other side of the lake." His disciples agreed, and they headed into the sunset. For the first few hours, the water was calm. There were no whitecaps. So Jesus went into the bow of the boat and lay down. Within minutes, He was fast asleep.

Suddenly, the skies grew dark and the wind started to blow. This was not an ordinary swell. It was a major storm cell development. The disciples were able to handle the challenge until the waves started to lap over the sides. Water began pouring into the boat, and no matter how fast they tried to bail it out, they couldn't stop the inundation.

Soon, they were gripped with panic. *This is not supposed to happen on a lake,* they thought. *This storm is going to kill us all.* Just before they were about to capsize, they ran to the belly of the boat and woke their Master. "Jesus, wake up! Wake up! The storm is too fierce. We're about to drown," they cried.

Jesus stood up, looked into the wind, and said, "Be quiet!" And to the waves He said, "Be still!" The elements did exactly as they were commanded. Everything became peaceful again.

The disciples were dumbfounded and full of awe. They said to one another, "Who in the world is this guy? He commands the sea and winds to obey Him, and they do."

I have looked at this passage of Scripture many times, asking myself, *Why was Jesus asleep?* I have come to two simple conclusions. First, He was asleep because He was tired. Jesus had worked hard all day, and His body was telling Him it was time for rest. Those who fly from one city to another often put their heads back and slip into Never Never Land before the plane pulls away from the gate. Why? Because they are tired.

Jesus was not only tired, but He had another reason for dozing off. I think He fell asleep because He had total assurance of one simple fact: He knew He was going to get to the other side. Not only did Jesus have a mission, but He had confidence too. This is something many of us lack. We might have direction. We might have a new lease on life. But it is imperative we have confidence in the mission, to keep us going in the right direction.

Notice what happened once the disciples woke Him up. Instead of thanking them for their startling wake-up call, He scolded them for their unbelief. Remember, these fishermen were experienced and knew how to read the signs of the weather. Imagine if a pilot and first officer came running out of the cockpit in the middle of a thunderstorm screaming, "Everyone, wake up! The plane is going down! We're all going to die!" It would cause mayhem in the hearts of everyone on board. The disciples were as skilled as anyone in their day, yet their hearts were filled with fear. The storm was fierce and succeeded in stealing their self-assurance. As a result, they lost their confidence that they were going to get to the other side. This is precisely what angered Jesus. In their minds they had reason to worry. In His mind, there was no reason to worry.

The difference between Christ and His disciples is clear. Although Jesus wasn't a skilled fisherman, He was an expert in faith and knew His destiny. His future was secure. The disciples felt no such confidence. For a brief few moments, they were filled with panic and lost touch with the great destiny of the kingdom Christ was promoting. They lost sight of the major role each of them would play in touching thousands and through the centuries millions upon millions of people.

Jesus did not rebuke them for their fear. He rebuked them for their lack of faith. Being concerned is one thing, and at times it is healthy. Fear and concern become detrimental when they begin to choke our vision of the future. The lesson for us is evident: Once we are convinced we are embracing the heart of God and have laid out His mission for our lives, we must stick to it, come what may. We must stay the course. Storms will form before our eyes. Earthquakes will shake us. Financial setbacks will come our way. Barriers will arise. In spite of all these things and in the midst of difficulty, struggle, and adversity, we must stay true to our missions. If we are faithful to God's heart and mission, He will stay true to us. If we partner with Christ, our boat will never sink.

## NO STORM LASTS FOREVER, NOT EVEN THE PERFECT ONE!

We began the process of change with the belief that, in the face of adversity and challenge, God wants the best for our lives. By this, I do not mean God wants what is easiest for us. He wants us to have challenging lives in which we learn and grow. I have never hoped or prayed that my daughters, whom I love deeply, would have an easy life. A life of ease would produce laziness. Instead, I want them to face and conquer the challenges in their childhoods that will prepare them for their adult lives. Please do not misunderstand. I do not want them to experience pain. I have no desire for them to experience anguish. But certain levels of resistance are necessary for growth. Much like a muscle grows from lifting weights, we grow as a result of facing challenges.

In the same way, God wants us, His children, to become all we can be. The only way we can reach our potential is by breaking through barriers. Barriers, by definition, are challenges. They are resistance. Since we believe God wants the best for us, we believe He wants us to gain victory over our challenges. There is no victory unless there is a battle. Easy lives have no battles, but neither do they have victories. They are what they are, the status quo, meaningless and boring.

Breaking barriers is not for wimps. Anytime we plan on realizing our greatest potential, we will face challenges. We will face adversity. How we manage ourselves through such difficulties will determine whether or not we reach our goals. In most cases our problems aren't our greatest challenges—how we face our problems in light of God's love for us determines whether or not we move beyond them.

I will never forget the day my daughter came home from school with a temperature of 102 degrees. We gave her some acetaminophen, but the fever never broke. My wife drove her to the clinic in downtown San José, Costa Rica. There, they told her our daughter had a urinary tract infection combined with strep throat. They said with some antibiotics she would be fine. The weekend passed, but her fever never dipped below 100.

At this point we became concerned. She was achy all over. Her throat was swollen and full of pain. In addition, she experienced a burning sensation when she went to the bathroom. We took her back to the clinic.

They took some blood tests, tested her level of antibodies, and prodded her ten-year-old body. The results were more than discouraging. She had appendicitis. On top of strep throat and the urinary tract infection, she would have to have an emergency appendectomy in the middle of the night. My heart sank.

After tucking our two other daughters into bed, I explained to them I had to go be with Celina and Mommy at the clinic. I told them Celina needed our prayers because she was going to have an operation. Our pastor's daughters lived across the street, and

I asked them to watch our girls during the operation. They kindly agreed.

I drove to the clinic about 9:30 p.m. Having the operation in a clinic in Central America didn't bother us. Being there without family did. The nearest relative lived thousands of miles away, and because of the urgency of the operation, no one could fly down in time.

I walked into the emergency room where the doctors had finished conducting their diagnosis. I asked for a few moments of privacy with my daughter. Pulling the curtain shut, I placed my hands on her little cheeks and gazed into her soft baby blue eyes. I will never forget the last thing I said to her: "Celina, I want you to know I love you." She nervously nodded. "The Lord loves you too!" Once again she nodded. "Celina, you are a good girl. You are a special girl. Everything is going to be fine. You are going to be fine." I squeezed her hands, pressed my cheek against hers, and prayed for her. Finally I kissed her forehead and said, "I'll see you when you get out."

The operation was scheduled to begin at 11:00 p.m. Another missionary couple joined us as we sat in the waiting area. To this day, I thank the Lord for them. They kept us laughing as we exchanged missionary horror stories.

At about 1:00 a.m., the doctor came out and said, "The operation went well. She is in the recovery room. Mr. Frenn, you can go home and get some rest." I turned to my wife and said, "If you feel comfortable, I'll head home to be with our girls." My wife stayed behind to be with Celina until the next day.

About 3:30 a.m., I received a call. It was my wife. She was crying with an edge of panic in her voice. She said, "Jason, I need to know if Celina has any history of breathing problems." I said, "No. Why?" She said, "The doctor left, and no one is around. She is having difficulty breathing, her lungs are filling up with fluid, and her kidneys are not functioning. Please pray. We need a miracle! Someone is coming. I need to go." Then she hung up.

No words can describe how I felt. Almost any attempt to explain my feelings would fall short of the reality of the moment. It was like my heart and lungs had been ripped out of my chest after being hit square in the face with a Louisville Slugger. I would have done anything to trade places with Celina.

I tried to call several family members to alert them to pray. There was no answer. I wouldn't have expected there to be. I called several friends in Costa Rica. Again, there was no answer. No matter whom I called, I got voice mail. I was stuck at home. There was nowhere to go, no one to help, no one to talk to. My wife was stranded at the hospital. She had no support, no one to talk to, and nowhere to go. The only thing connecting us was a cell phone. I had a car, but my girls were fast asleep and I couldn't leave them.

I walked into Celina's empty bedroom. Her bed was made up with teddy bears nicely aligned. I knelt at her bedside and made another call. This time, I called upon the Lord. He is Someone I can always call. No matter how many times we call, no matter what time of day it is, He always answers. He never fails. When we call on the name of the Lord, we are never sent to voice mail.

I am not a sensationalist, nor am I prone to blow things out of proportion. Still, it felt as though the Lord Himself knelt right next to me and started to intercede for my daughter. This is what the Bible says in Romans 8:34: "Christ Jesus, who died—more than that, who was raised to life—is at the right hand of God and is also interceding for us" (NIV). What a great privilege to be able to go to the Lord in times of need. Jesus intercedes for us. In my moment of crisis, He put His arm around me, and we prayed together for my daughter. Although there was nothing to see through my physical eyes, something happened in those fifteen minutes of intense prayer. Toward the end, an overwhelming peace came over me. This was when my wife called for the second time.

She said, "Celina is still having difficulty breathing, but she has stabilized. They are moving her to a private room." No, we were not out of the woods. But the word *stabilized* was encouraging, and the peace this gave me allowed me to sleep for an hour and a half. Early that morning I put my other girls on the school bus and headed to the clinic.

The tableaux awaiting me in my daughter's hospital room was stunning. Against the wall stood Paul and Karla Weis, our area directors. Both had tears in their eyes. Against the other wall stood my wife. All were staring at the small body that lay in the bed with every imaginable tube stuck into her. The doctors had attached a catheter, an IV, a tab placed over her fingertips to measure blood oxygen levels, and scores of wires monitoring her heart, while they administered a cocktail of antibiotics to fight off her bronchial pneumonia. She looked as white as a ghost.

With tears streaming down my face, I called her name and stroked her wet hair. Her skin was clammy and had no color. She struggled for each breath. Her chest expanded at a pace of thirty breaths per minute.

As the day progressed, friends began to pour in. Many relatives called, and the word spread: our daughter needed God's help. People all over the globe began to pray for her. This was a crucial morning, and Cindee and I are eternally grateful to those who prayed with us through those difficult eight hours. Though they were not present, they were with us in spirit.

At about 10:00 a.m., our family practitioner, who hadn't been present during the operation, came into the room. He said, "I really cannot say anything, but I think something went wrong when they administered liquid during the procedure. Obviously, there was no control, and she came close to drowning."

That evening, the two surgeons came in. One said, "First, I want to thank both of you for how well you have handled the situation. Most parents would have lost control by now. Most parents would have been screaming and threatening a malpractice suit. But both of you have managed this storm well."

I said, "Tell me, Doctor, what went wrong? Why didn't anyone know she was developing pneumonia?"

He said, "We normally check for it, but unfortunately, we didn't. We have no answers. I am truly sorry." We responded, "She has stabilized, and God intervened. That is the important thing now."

That night, my wife went home for a good night's sleep. I stayed at the hospital with our daughter and stared at her little body as it struggled for each breath for several hours. At about 7:00 p.m., the doctors removed the catheter along with all the wires, except for the oxygen monitor and IV. The doctors wanted her to get up and try walking to the bathroom. She stubbornly said, "I don't want to go to the bathroom."

I said, "Honey, you need to try. Besides, the doctors say you need to get the blood moving a bit."

She shook her head in frustration and said, "Whatever."

It took about five laborious minutes to get her ready for the ten-foot journey. She was in significant pain. With each step came a justifiable moan. When she stepped into the bathroom, she turned and said in an aggressive tone, "I should have never come to this hospital! Look at me!"

Full of sadness and grief, I looked down and shared something from my heart. I said, "Sweetheart, I am so sorry. If we had never become missionaries, you might not be in this mess. Perhaps if we had never boarded the aircraft and moved to Central America, then maybe this would have never happened to you."

Her countenance changed, and she confidently replied, "Oh, Daddy, don't say that. I love being a missionary. I love this country. I hate this hospital, but I love being a missionary." Within five seconds, my daughter set me straight on the priorities of life. She realigned my point of view. Suddenly, I gained a whole new perspective in the midst of the storm. I found God's course again.

I learned an important lesson: No storm lasts forever, not even the perfect one. Instead of avoiding pain at all cost, the better road is to find a way of managing how we face it. Pain is unavoidable. It will always be a part of life. How we face the barrier, however, will determine whether or not we break it. There is no better way to face challenges than to do so with God. He does not want us to have an easy life, but rather a meaningful and significant life. This implies that growth will always be part of the process. It means barriers must be broken. They must be overcome! It means God wants us to break through them, not avoid them.

People continued to visit and check on our daughter's recovery over the four days Celina was in the hospital. Within that time, her lungs cleared of all fluid. The doctors said they had never seen such a miraculous recovery from a case of pneumonia that severe. Yes, there was a miracle. Her lungs had experienced healing. Indeed, her recovery was miraculous. Over those four days and with much prayer, the hand of the Lord brought healing to her body. There were other breakthroughs aside from the physical healing as seen by the human eye. Perhaps the most prominent one was a change of perspective in how I view the barriers I face.

The truth is I don't want to see any of my children in this

condition ever again. I don't wish that on anyone. However, I realized one simple truth through this difficulty. Without this painful experience, I wouldn't be who I am today. Celina wouldn't be who she is today. My perspective on serving the Lord in a foreign country wouldn't be what it is today. I realize now in a very personal way that God doesn't want life to be easy. He wants it to be meaningful. He wants us to move beyond barriers and become all we can be.

Today, our daughter is a well-adjusted teenager who is highly dedicated to her relationship with the Lord. She joyfully serves in ministry and harbors no resentment or anger. Years later, the only negative reminder of her difficult time in the hospital is a two-and-a-half-inch scar where the doctors removed her appendix.

As you read this book, I hope you don't think I am forecasting disaster for your life. On the contrary, I want to see you blessed with a life full of significance. And I hope you understand that as you begin to reach your greatest potential, you will hit barriers. Expect obstacles. Expect times of pain. How you face such adversity will determine whether or not you reach the great destiny that awaits you.

There is no obstacle too big. There is no barrier too overwhelming. There is no setback too large. There is no day of suffering too great. No matter how intense the storm, it won't last. It never does.

I believe a new dawn awaits you. Perhaps your child is sick or your marriage is failing. Perhaps your job promotion is out of reach. Maybe your dream house is unattainable and too costly. No matter what the barrier is, no matter what obstacle you're facing, a new day is coming!

God, the Author of life, looks at you with excitement and anticipation. He is waiting to work in you, His creation, to overcome the issues holding you back and fulfill His wonderful call upon your life.

In the previous chapter, we worked together to form a godly heart. In this chapter, we carved out a mission statement. No matter what circumstances we find ourselves in, God will help us plot a course that is both significant and meaningful, a course that is meaningful not only for us but also for those with whom we come in contact. Our mission statement will guide us toward victory and the great destiny God intends for our lives. When you get up each morning, remind yourself of your golden thread, and live it every day!

Congratulations, the first pillar is in place. You're on your way to a great victory!

The next two chapters deal with godly wisdom, which is the second pillar. Godly wisdom gives us the ability to make good decisions in harmony with our godly missions. Wisdom helps us decide the best course of action to accomplish our goals. With God's help, we will see great progress in overcoming the barriers that hold us back.

God loves us and wants the best for our lives. As we close this chapter together, let's pray the following prayer. The Lord will honor your desire to implement what you have learned in this chapter.

*Dear Lord, thank You for giving me the gift of life. I realize You have created life full of purpose, meaning, and significance. Create in me Your godly heart as I attempt to develop a godly mission statement. I know You have called me to a purpose and destiny. Help me to take the first step in breaking the barriers as I write out Your golden thread for my life.*

*I need Your help to discover my lifetime goal and move toward it with great courage and conviction. Help me to judge all choices by my lifetime goal so I may stay the course. In times of crisis and adversity, help me to know You are there and You will see me through to the other side. I ask for Your guidance, direction, and steadfastness in Jesus' name. Amen.*

The Wisdom of

The Father    The Son

Sound Judgment

Fear & Respect        Knowledge        Creativity
Godly Perspective     Godly Sense      New Paradigms

## The Wisdom of the Son

*God has provided wisdom through the example of His Son, Jesus Christ. Of all the people in the Bible, Christ was the wisest and displayed His wisdom with great humility and grace. He faced ministerial, social, and political barriers every day. With poise He debated the authorities, taught the multitudes, and blessed the poor.*

*In times of adversity and confusion, the wisdom of Christ helps us make good decisions that are harmonious with our missions. Godly wisdom helps us judge every decision we make in the light of our godly missions. I call this the second pillar. It connects seamlessly to the heart of the Father (the first pillar) and takes us one step closer to breaking the barriers and becoming all that God has destined us to be.*

# CHAPTER 4

# Making Godly Sense

I N June 2004, Cindee, the girls, and I were wrapping up another four-year term of missionary service in Central America. We moved out of our house, put everything in storage, and headed to a hotel two days before our departure. Upon our arrival in the hotel lobby, we asked the bellhop to store four pieces of luggage in their storage facility.

Sound asleep at 4:30 a.m., I received the famous wake-up call from the hotel operator, jolting me out of a coma and telling me it was time to get up and head to the airport. We were all exhausted because we had been to a Quinceañera (a coming-out party for girls fifteen years of age in Latin America) the night before. Stumbling out of our room just before 5:00 a.m., we barely made the shuttle for the airport. We were excited to head home, on a flight from Costa Rica to Los Angeles.

Our check-in was surprisingly smooth. We moved through security swiftly. Arriving at our gate, we dropped our carry-on luggage and sat down for a twenty-five-minute rest. Wanting one last piece of Costa Rica, Chanel, our middle child, turned to Cindee with a tear in her eye and asked if she could go to the kiosk to get one last order of rice and beans. I gave her the money, and she headed off. Jazmin, in the meantime, fell asleep next to her back-pack and carry-on.

At 6:35 a.m., the announcement came: "All passengers, please proceed to gate four to begin immediate boarding." We walked down the long ramp and boarded the 757 that would take us back to our homeland. Everything went off without a hitch. Everyone boarded quickly. The girls were situated three rows in front of us. We pulled back from the gate five minutes ahead of schedule. *L.A., here we come,* I thought.

As we approached the end of the runway after taxiing, we waited about seven minutes to be cleared for takeoff.

The airline on which we were flying allows passengers to hear the conversations between the pilots and the control tower. I must admit, I am an addict when it comes to this service. I enjoy hearing every transmission in and out of the cockpit. So at the time, I was listening to the transmissions.

All of a sudden, I heard something that got my attention. The control tower called our aircraft and said, "We have a bag that did not make the flight. The owner is a Mr. Jason Brent." Ever since I have lived in Central America, few have pronounced my name correctly, but I was pretty sure they meant me. . . . One of *my* bags didn't make the flight. I thought this was strange because we had been among the first ones to check in.

The pilot replied, "I understand the bag will make the flight tomorrow." The control tower replied, "Affirmative . . . please stand by." Several long minutes passed. There we waited at the end of the runway, and I knew one of my bags would not make the international flight. The airline would have to deliver it to our address in Los Angeles.

Then the control tower said, "The aircraft cannot be cleared for departure, because the OIJ [the Costa Rican FBI] has been called in to look at the suspicious bag. Please stand by." All of a sudden, my normal blood pressure went from 120/80 to about 150/90.

*Please stand by,* I thought. *I don't want to stand by. What in the world is happening to my bag, and why is the OIJ examining it?*

Then the control tower said, "It seems as though they have labeled this particular piece of luggage as a bomb threat. The local authorities want the passenger to disembark. Please stand by." At that moment I think my blood pressure must have hit 180/110. About two more minutes passed before the head flight attendant made an announcement over the PA system: "Mr. Jason Brent, please identify yourself by pushing the yellow call button above your seat."

I waited a few seconds in case there really *was* a Jason Brent, but all the while I knew they were looking for me, Jason Frenn. All one hundred-plus passengers were anxiously waiting to see this Mr. Jason Brent identify himself. I took a deep breath. I raised my hand in slow motion. I reached up and pushed the little orange button with a symbol of a flight attendant carrying a food tray. I must admit I was afraid someone would come with cuffs instead. As I pushed the button, the sound seemed to drop an octave or two. Instead of a friendly *bing,* it sounded like an ominous *bong.*

Instantly, I was connected to the crime. There was no doubt. There was no more wondering who the guilty party was. Everyone who had heard the conversation between the control tower and our pilots positively ID'd me with the words "bomb threat." I went from a normal everyday traveling guy to a third-world terrorist in about two seconds.

The flight attendant came back with a rather serious look on her face. She said, "Are you Jason Brent?"

I replied, "No, my name is Jason Frenn. I heard the conversations with the pilots and the control tower, and I am really sorry about all the mix-up."

She said, "We've been told to wait."

Fifteen minutes passed before finally the tower replied, "We have received another update from the authorities. They definitely want the passenger to disembark and identify his bag." By now, of course, everyone in the plane was listening to the radio transmissions.

My mind started to race. Questions and doubts ran rapidly through my head: *What could it be? What could have possibly triggered the authorities to ground the aircraft and force me off the plane with the suspicion I had planted a bomb? What could be in one of our bags to make them think of a terrorist attack?*

Then I remembered that while we stayed at the hotel the night before, four of our bags were kept in a storage facility in the hotel lobby. I turned to my wife and said, "Were our bags locked or sealed while stored at the hotel?"

She replied, "I didn't even think about it."

I thought, *I bet someone planted something in one of our pieces of luggage during our time in the room. The person obviously knew I would never check. And as a result, I will be thrown into a Costa Rican jail for the rest of my life. No matter what happens, this is going to be real ugly.*

It might not have been someone from the hotel. Maybe our iMac computer triggered something on their X-ray machine. Maybe it was the twelve-volt transformer or some other electronic device we were taking back with us.

While I drowned in a cesspool of paranoia and mind games, the captain turned the plane around and headed back to the terminal. Before arriving at a gate, however, the plane was diverted to an isolated place about a hundred yards from the terminal.

The plane came to a stop, and the engines were shut down. The flight attendant came back and asked me to head to the front of the aircraft.

James 1:5 says, "If any of you lacks wisdom, he should ask God, who gives generously to all without finding fault, and it will be given to him" (NIV). That's exactly what I did. I was in a bind. I had no idea what to do, and I was scared. So I asked the Lord, "God, what should I do? I need *Your* wisdom."

One simple question came to my mind. It turned out to be the wisest question of the week. As the flight attendant escorted me to the front, I asked, "Would the pilot be willing to accompany me off the aircraft?" Looking somewhat puzzled she replied, "Well, I guess we can ask him."

Sometimes the wisest thing we can do is ask a simple question. The attendant knocked on the cockpit door and a tall, well-groomed pilot answered. She said, "Captain, Mr. Frenn would like you to accompany him to the terminal." He smiled and said, "That would be fine."

At first, it was awkward as we patiently waited for the ground crew to open the aircraft door. It felt like being in an elevator when everyone just stares at the blinking numbers indicating which floor they're passing.

Finally I broke the silence. "If for some reason I cannot get back onto the plane, my wife and children are traveling with me."

He said, "I know. I tried to tell the authorities, but they refused to listen to me." This surprised me. Apparently, he knew all about us before he parked the airplane.

He said, "What do you do?"

I said, "We are missionaries."

"Oh, that is great," he replied.

"Further, I am an ordained minister," I said.

He jokingly rolled his eyes, as if to say sarcastically, "Well, you're obviously a security risk."

Suddenly I had an ally, a very powerful and respected ally.

When the ground crew and the authorities opened the door and saw that the pilot was going with me, their demeanor changed. With respect and courtesy they escorted us into a minivan that took us back to the main terminal. We exited the vehicle, and the airline personnel smiled and said, "Please head up the stairs adjacent to the Jetway." We walked up the stairs and down the ramp to the same gate through which we had boarded the aircraft an hour and thirty minutes earlier. What could have been a scenario in which I was taken into custody to *who knows where,* was turning into a VIP luggage-recovery operation.

I thought, *This is strange. Why don't they take me downstairs where the luggage and cargo facilities are? Why aren't we heading to some interrogator's office? Perhaps the authorities have offices in the main terminal where all the departure gates are.*

In essence, we were backtracking our original steps. They were the very same steps we took when we originally boarded the aircraft. We headed down the same tunnel, walked past the same person who took our boarding passes, and came back to the same gate. As I looked across the gate area, I noticed a carry-on bag sitting in the midst of a circle of security personnel. It was the black carry-on my daughter had been pulling behind her until we sat down for those brief twenty-five minutes before boarding the flight.

Suddenly my nerves started to calm rather quickly. I blurted, "Hey, that's my daughter's carry-on. I'm so sorry. It must have been left behind. Forgive me for the inconvenience. Would you like me to open it?"

Unanimously they said, "Please do," as they cautiously took about five steps back.

I opened the carry-on and pulled out a blow dryer, a curling iron, some small packets of makeup, and a couple of other toiletries. I said, "Do you need to see anything else?"

They said, "No."

I asked them if they had taken their liberty to inspect the bag. They said they hadn't. I asked if they had bomb-sniffing dogs. They replied, "Yes, but we didn't want to bother to have them brought up to inspect the bag. We felt it would be best to have you come, claim the bag, and open it yourself."

The captain was a bit upset that they hadn't destroyed the bag an hour before. I was relieved but embarrassed. He and I turned and headed back to the aircraft. I had never contemplated the serious repercussions of an abandoned piece of luggage in an airport, even luggage as innocent as a daughter's carry-on. In the minivan I said, "I guess I owe everyone an apology." He said, "You don't owe anyone anything. Tell them your bag was cleared. That is what I am going to tell everyone. Don't worry about it."

Once I got onto the plane, I faced more than one hundred passengers, some anxiously wondering if I was a terrorist. I think the most shocking thing for them was watching a passenger not only forced to identify a very questionable piece of luggage, but also getting back onto the plane with yet another bag and storing it in the overhead compartment. Ironic, isn't it?

After seven hours of travel and one stop in Guatemala, we landed one hour and fifteen minutes behind schedule in Los Angeles. Scores of passengers missed their connecting flights. Needless to say, none of them were pleased with me. The twenty minutes we spent standing around the baggage claim carousel were very uncomfortable.

Finally the luggage began to roll in, and a young blond teenager accompanied by her friend wandered over to the spot where I was standing. She crossed her arms and shook her head in disgust. Then she turned to me and said, "I can't believe I missed my connecting flight. This has thrown a huge monkey wrench into my schedule. I would love to meet the *idiot* who left his bag in the San José airport and caused us this enormous delay."

At that, her friend tried to stop her and forcefully whispered into her ear, "Shhhh, that's him. That's the idiot!"

She immediately turned red. I calmly turned to her and said, "That'd be me."

Without a small dose of wisdom, the outcome of that incident could have been entirely different. Wisdom knocked on my door at the most crucial time in the story. When did it come? It came after I asked God for it. As the authorities were sending a car to take me back to the terminal, I politely asked the pilot to accompany me to see what the problem was. When he kindly agreed to escort me, my nerves began to settle. My heart stopped racing. All of a sudden, I was able to think without being paranoid. I felt more secure instead of out of control. I was able to communicate without running at the mouth. Most important, wisdom gave me an ally, an ally who knew the rules. And I knew one simple fact: as long as the pilot was by my side, that aircraft wasn't going anywhere!

Being wise gives us the ability to ask the right questions and the skill to make sound decisions. In the midst of my storm, a simple petition proved to be the wisest thing I did the entire week.

When you're facing a situation that seems hopeless, ask the Lord for wisdom. He is more than willing to give you the wisdom to effectively overcome your barriers.

## TRUE WISDOM

In the two previous chapters we established the first pillar in our quest to break the barriers and become all we are destined to be. The first pillar is the creation of a heart that is godly, full of virtue and decency. In essence, building the first pillar means seeing the heart of God and taking steps to make it our own. This gives us the moral compass we need when barriers and adversity arise. Once we take on God's character, we begin to establish the second pillar: the wisdom of the Son.

Wisdom can be defined several ways. It is the accumulation of knowledge gained through experience. It is commonly defined as the knowledge and experience needed to make sensible decisions and judgments. It is the good sense shown by the decisions and judgments we make.

Many people around the world use common sense and make sound judgments. Wisdom can be seen in every law, religion, and social norm. Our parents have it. Our grandparents have it. Our second-grade teacher has it. So what distinguishes wisdom and common sense from the wisdom of God? The wisdom of God is a step above all other forms of common sense and wisdom.

The Lord states in Isaiah 55:8, "My thoughts are not your thoughts, neither are your ways my ways" (NIV). What sets His wisdom miles above our own? He is the Designer of the universe. He knows the intricacies of every atom of every molecule of every cell of every organism. He is the Author of the genetic code.

He makes the rules, and, most important, He is the Designer of all wisdom. Godly wisdom gives us the ability to make decisions and have sound judgment based upon His perspective. In essence, it gives us the ability to see the world from a heavenly perspective. Godly wisdom gives us what we need to make decisions and judgments even when they might not make sense to us.

Why is godly wisdom so important? Some might say, "Isn't common sense good enough? Isn't ordinary reasoning sufficient?" The answer is yes if you want to be common, ordinary, and mediocre. In order to break the barriers, overcome adversity, and reach our greatest potential, we must see the barriers from a godly perspective.

God is best defined by two powerful adjectives. First, He is *omnipotent*. This means He possesses unlimited power and authority. He calls the shots. He makes the rules. He is subject to none. He yields to no one. When He decides something will have a certain outcome, there is no alternate ending. It's something He sees and knows before it ever occurs.

Second, God is *omnipresent*. This means He is present in every given moment, including ten thousand years ago and ten thousand years from now. God knows the outcome and the ramifications of every decision ever made. He can see the creation of the world as well as its end simultaneously. And He is present in every microsecond in between. Because He can see all things at all times in all places, God's perspective is balanced and true beyond any human ability. God's perspective is perfect, unchanging, and never failing. Therefore, if we partner with Him, He offers us the greatest source for insight and decision-making power.

If we want to break barriers, doesn't it follow that we must tap into the great wisdom Christ offers us? Only then will we be able to reach our greatest potential. Because of His omnipotence and omnipresence, He sees things from every point of view. Simply put, He owns all perspective. This is what distinguishes the wisdom of God from common sense.

## THERE IS NO BENCHMARK,
## JUST A STARTING PLACE

In my preparation for writing this book, I pored over many reference works, trying to find a standard for measuring wisdom. I wanted to find a measurement test that would help you understand your areas of strength and weakness. To my dismay, I made a startling discovery. Unlike IQ tests found in every corner of the globe, there are no wisdom tests. There are no standards. There are no benchmarks. Why is that? Unlike IQ, wisdom embraces not just knowledge but judgment as well, and sound judgment is very difficult to measure.

Many of us are caught behind barriers not because of a lack of knowledge but because of poor judgment. In this world there are many people who are good. However, few are good and wise. Few understand the great importance of wisdom and the role it must play if we want to break the barriers that hinder us. So where do we begin?

Our starting point must be what the Bible calls "the beginning of wisdom." Psalm 111:10 says, "The fear of the LORD is the beginning of wisdom; all who follow his precepts have good understanding" (NIV). The word *fear* in this context does not mean paranoia, anxiety, terror, or panic. Rather, it means respect for or awe of somebody or something. In other words, respect for the Lord and appreciation of His omnipotence are the starting point for acquiring His wisdom.

God has engineered us to learn from the things and people we respect the most. We gain knowledge from those we respect and admire. If we have a fearful respect for God, then we will learn from Him and take on His wisdom.

## THE FEAR FACTOR

I was desperately looking for a church. Fear had filled my heart and had been building over a period of a couple of days. For the first time in my life, I had an overwhelming insecurity about my spiritual destination in eternity. I had no idea if I was going to heaven or hell.

At the time, I was ten years of age. Most of my few church experiences had been in a foreign language: Arabic. My grandmother would take me to mass in North Hollywood to a church filled with Lebanese immigrants. Because of the language barrier, I knew very little about spiritual things, and I was biblically ignorant.

For some reason, questions of heaven and hell began to storm my mind. Perhaps it was a movie I had seen or a passing conversation I had overheard. Either way, I was terrified I would wind up in hell. No matter what I did to distract myself, my anxiety continued to escalate, an overwhelming sensation for a ten-year-old child.

The Saturday after my anxiety began, I told my mom I desperately needed to go to a church. I explained my fear of hell and how I needed to connect with God to avoid the black abyss that swallows ten-year-old boys.

My mom was not a churchgoer, but she felt sorry for me. We called our neighbors who religiously attended each Saturday night service. I asked if I could go with them the same Saturday night. They kindly agreed.

Seven of us piled into a car large enough to be the twin of the *Titanic*. The 1970 Oldsmobile was good enough transportation for me. All I wanted was to arrive in one piece and clear up any differences I may have had with the One who holds the keys to the pearly gates.

When we walked into the majestic Catholic church, I was impressed by the splendor and beautiful decor. The greatest impression of the fifty-five-minute experience, however, was the overwhelming sense that I was safe, protected, and in a good place.

I remember kneeling with five hundred other parishioners and repeating prayers that resonated in my heart for the first time. I thought, *Heaven is a good, safe place. All I need to do is make sure I am in good standing with the Big Man upstairs, and everything is going to be just fine.* My fearful respect for the Lord translated into the first wise step in my spiritual walk. Kneeling in the church, I asked the Lord for forgiveness of any sin I had committed against Him. I experienced peace.

Indeed, everything was going to be fine. That experience was the beginning of godly wisdom for me. I lived out what it means to fear the Lord. I realized I was dealing with the almighty God, and I needed to align my will to His. If an eight-hundred-pound gorilla can sit anywhere he wants, then the Almighty can do whatever He wants, whenever and however He pleases. And wisdom began when I yielded my will to His.

Jesus says in Matthew 10:28, "Do not be afraid of those who kill the body but cannot kill the soul. Rather, be afraid of the One who can destroy both soul and body in hell" (NIV). This night, I recognized I needed to be in alliance with the One who had power over all who might enter heaven or hell. It was an experience with a profound impact that has lasted until the present day.

My respect for the Lord has only increased over the years. My reverence for Him has grown as well. As a result, I no longer worry about winding up in hell. I no longer have any anxiety about my spiritual destination in eternity. Wisdom was birthed in my life because of my fear of and respect for the Lord.

## R-E-S-P-E-C-T

How can you build respect for the Lord? You can start by contemplating His omnipotence and omnipresence. Think about His power and greatness. Meditate on His sovereignty and the awesomeness of His creation.

In 1999, my family went to the Grand Canyon. As our car approached a clearing in the trees, our view of the largest carved chasm in the United States was overwhelming, to say the least. When we stood at the edge and looked across the first segment of the enormous canyon, I realized "canyon" is a term that falls far short of its meaning. There is no word to adequately describe the immensity of the Grand Canyon.

It's a mile from the top of the ravine to the river floor. In some spots, it measures eighteen miles wide. It totals more than 1.2 million acres or 1,904 square miles. Within its walls, the river stretches more than 277 miles. A trip through the Grand Canyon by raft can take two weeks or longer.

Indeed it is an awesome sight. Well, the God of the universe created not only the Grand Canyon but also the entire world—in a day. Contemplate His creation, His greatness, and His power. Contemplate that He is everywhere at all times, and you will develop a new respect for Him.

## PEOPLE AND PROVERBS

Once you have laid a foundation of respect for the Lord, wisdom will follow. But you may ask, "How do I grow godly wisdom in my life?" There are two important elements necessary for growing in godly wisdom: people and proverbs. Spending time with people who have godly wisdom affects our lives in a powerful way.

Provided our hearts are open, we cannot help but be influenced by their example. Furthermore, studying the Proverbs on a regular basis guides us biblically so that we are not swayed by the winds that might carry us off course. Both people and proverbs play an important part in the process of breaking barriers, overcoming adversity, and reaching our greatest potential. First, let's focus on the importance of associating with people who embrace godly wisdom.

Surrounding ourselves with people who have godly wisdom helps us grow in godly wisdom. "Birds of a feather flock together" is a common expression that implies we become like those with whom we spend time. This is true for better or for worse.

If we hang out with people who are racists, we may well begin to reflect those values. If we spend too much time with those who struggle with addiction, we too may see a struggle beginning to develop in our lives. Likewise, if we spend time with those who do good, we too will begin to do good to others. The values of those with whom we spend time have an effect on our lives.

The same is true in regard to wisdom. If we spend time with those who are wise and see things from a godly perspective, then we will learn from them and grow in the godly wisdom they have learned. Proverbs 13:20 says, "He who walks with the wise grows wise, but a companion of fools suffers harm" (NIV). As we set out in search of Christ's wisdom, we must surround ourselves with people who value and pursue God's wisdom. Then we will make decisions as they do, *wise* decisions.

Think about the people you spend the most time with. Who are they? Do these people reflect the kind of person you want to become? Do they edify you? Do they pull you up instead of tear you down?

Here is what the Bible says:

*Do not be yoked together with unbelievers. For what do righteousness and wickedness have in common? Or what fellowship can light have with darkness?* (2 Corinthians 6:14 NIV)

*Confess your sins to each other and pray for each other so that you may be healed. The prayer of a righteous man is powerful and effective.* (James 5:16 NIV)

*Live in harmony with one another; be sympathetic, love as brothers, be compassionate and humble.* (1 Peter 3:8 NIV)

*Do not forget to do good and to share with others, for with such sacrifices God is pleased. Obey your leaders and submit to their authority. They keep watch over you as men who must give an account. Obey them so that their work will be a joy, not a burden, for that would be of no advantage to you.* (Hebrews 13:16–17 NIV)

In choosing the people with whom we surround ourselves, we must look past the superficial trappings that attract us to them for the wrong reasons. Instead, we need to examine their actions, reputations, and values. We ought to pay attention to how they are regarded and whether they are respected. We should ask whether they are suitable candidates for modeling godly wisdom. The people with whom we choose to spend time, and to whom we look for insight and respect, can have a large impact on whether or not we become godly people. For this reason, it is essential to measure them accurately and choose friends carefully.

## IT COULD HAVE BEEN ME

The first night of my debut crusade was traumatic, to say the least. It was held in a marginalized community, and more than 50 percent of those in attendance were gang members. Close to six hundred people filled the small lot located near the heart of all the drug activity in the town.

Ten minutes after the program started, a few of the gang members started hurtling huge concrete rocks that exploded on our aluminum stage. Several brawls broke out, and when we called the police, they said they would not come out until the next afternoon. We knew we were on our own.

By the third night, the danger had grown even more. An undercover police officer arrested a drug dealer who was trying to sell him cocaine. When the man resisted arrest, two other undercover cops came out of nowhere and beat him to the ground with nunchakus. His face was covered with blood when they threw him into the back of the squad car and took him to jail.

During the fourth and final night, another fight broke out. A young man struck someone from an enemy gang with a crowbar square in the forehead, nearly splitting his skull in two. The victim fell to the ground. Scores converged on one another, but the injured individual along with his gang were no match for the overwhelming presence of the other band of hoodlums.

Several gathered around their fallen comrade and carried him off the lot while the others fled. They explained what had happened to the rest of their gang, who happened to be several blocks away in front of a local bar. Within minutes they returned in greater numbers.

I will never forget the scene that unfolded before my eyes. Fifteen men walked onto the lot led by the five most feared drug dealers in that community. These were the five leaders of organized crime in the region. When their feet touched the lot, it was like placing a drop of liquid soap into a pot filled with greasy water. Everyone scattered. For the first time in my life, I saw an entire crowd move out of the way to give five men a clear path.

They began to scan the lot, looking for the young man who had the crowbar. Little did they know, he had disappeared. But they kept looking for him in the crowd of six hundred. At the end of the service, they confessed to me they had plotted to destroy our campaign and planned to harm me as well. Something happened, however, that prevented their evil plan. One of the ushers walked up to them and began to confront their lifestyle of crime and delinquency. When we closed the service, all of them prayed a simple prayer asking the Lord to forgive them for their wrongdoings.

One of them went home with a seed of change in his heart. His name was Miguel. He confessed to me that he had been one of those throwing large concrete rocks the first night, which had nearly ruined our event.

Many lives were touched and transformed at that event. Hundreds of lives were changed for all eternity. But I do not know how many experienced the radical transformation Miguel did. Little did he know, over the course of the next several years, his life would never be the same.

Miguel lived in a home filled with conflict, agony, and hostility. It was a humble abode located in the heart of the community, several blocks from our first crusade. In a town where the average income was less than one hundred dollars per month, his family was not exempt from financial struggles. The small structure they lived in was home to six.

Family dysfunction characterized Miguel's home life. Miguel's father was an alcoholic and physically abused his mother. Several of Miguel's brothers had been incarcerated. His older brother had struggled with drugs.

One night, when Miguel was younger, his father came home in a drunken rage. Several neighbors heard the screaming as he forced both his son and his wife into the street at knifepoint. They were anguished over being ripped out of their beds and thrown into the streets in the middle of the night. They sat on the curb outside their home completely humiliated until a neighbor took them in for the night.

The destructive pattern of abuse was a regular occurrence in their household. Each night when Miguel's dad came home, they wondered what might trigger another nightmare. The craziness grew with time.

Alcoholism is a destructive force that not only affects the ones who drink, but also everyone connected to the home. The consequences can be demoralizing, devastating, and even fatal.

On one occasion, his parents had a terrible argument. His father struck Miguel's mom with such force it knocked her unconscious. The blow caused an aneurysm in her brain. They rushed her to the hospital, but there was little hope. The doctors consulted with each other and finally operated. Both Miguel and his father sat in the waiting room, hoping for some good news.

To their grave disappointment, there was none. The head surgeon came into the waiting area and said, "I am sorry, but your wife is not going to make it. At best, she is going to be a vegetable. We recommend you take her home in the next several days so she can die there. This will be best for her." Miguel and his father felt completely destroyed. The news was devastating. Of course Miguel's father felt extremely guilty for the consequences of his alcoholism.

They took her home. Her head was shaved. Her skin was pale. Her body was weak. Their hopes were diminished. They laid her in her bed and waited. A week passed, but her condition hardly changed. Yet, for some reason, God spared her life.

She drifted in and out of consciousness. Within weeks of her return home, someone came to the door with a flyer announcing a crusade coming to their neighborhood. The top of the flyer read, "Hay Esperanza en Jesús," which is translated, "There is hope in Jesus." With a weak voice and mustering the strength to look into Miguel's eyes, she said, "Llévame a la cruzada de mi hermano Jason." Which means, "Take me to brother Jason's crusade." How could they say no? How could they deny her? Her husband felt guilty and was willing to do anything for her.

Finally, it was the last night of the crusade. The anticipated moment of her encounter with God came on a Saturday night. They drove her to the crusade located on a large community soccer field.

Somehow she endured the loud music, cold conditions, and user-*un*friendly seating arrangements. In those days, we had no crowd control, no chairs, and no aisles, just a crowd of five thousand standing for three hours. But she wasn't there for the music or a good place to sit. She didn't come that night because of the weather. She came to the crusade to ask for prayer.

When I gave the altar call, her loved ones escorted her to the front. At the time, I didn't know the details of her condition. I only knew by the signaling of those around her that she needed a miracle. According to her testimony, after praying that night, God touched her.

She said she felt better almost instantaneously. By the end of the evening, she was able to walk the distance back to her home, which was three quarters of a mile. God *had* touched her. Indeed, she had experienced a miracle. To this day, the doctors are baffled.

There was no logical explanation for her recovery other than a miracle.

And she wasn't the only one to experience a miracle this night. Her family experienced one too, and as a result, they made a radical shift from destructive behavior to constructive behavior. Miguel and his mother began to go to church. Miguel's father began to go as well and even began to attend Alcoholics Anonymous meetings.

Instead of spending time with those who were proponents of destruction, violence, and abuse, Miguel started to befriend those who were wise. He separated himself from the folly and foolishness of those who lived destructive and delinquent lifestyles. His new friends helped him build new and healthy patterns. They helped him steer clear of patterns of destruction.

Three years after his mother's healing, Miguel came and volunteered for another outreach. He helped set up the lights, sound, and stage. He ran the spotlights each night. My crusade logistics coordinator was impressed and asked Miguel to travel with us on our nationwide tour. Within a year, he was working for us full-time, setting up the same platform he had tried to destroy several years before. Soon he was in charge of many of the logistics pertaining to crusades reaching tens of thousands of people on a monthly basis.

Our team poured into his life. We discipled him. We helped him see things from God's perspective and taught him that with God's wisdom he could overcome any obstacle and break any barrier in his path. I counseled him personally on many occasions, and he listened to and heeded our guidance.

One day, he came into my office. He looked white as a ghost as he said, "I need to talk with you." He said, "On my way to work today, I was walking across a vacant lot. I discovered two bare feet coming up out of the ground. I called the police, and they came out to investigate."

He continued, "They uncovered the body of one of the gang members I knew when I was younger. He was someone I used to hang out with. He was wearing no clothes and was buried upside down. Obviously, this was a drug deal gone bad. I have a feeling I know who did this." Although this was alarming, it wasn't what was troubling him.

He paused for a second and explained what was disturbing him. Gazing at the floor of my office he said, "It could have been me. If it hadn't been for the changes God has made in my life, it could have been me buried in the lot." The stark realization stared him square in the face. He could see how the choices he had made based upon godly wisdom not only set him on a different path but also saved his life.

Any one of us could probably ask the question, "How drastically different would my life be if it weren't for the changes God has performed in me?" How about your life, friend? Is your life different because of the godly choices you've made? Have you given God the freedom to work in your life?

Miguel was correct. If he hadn't experienced the life-changing power of Christ, he might have ended up like the gang member buried naked with his feet sprouting out of the ground like daisies in a dirt lot. But he made wise choices in spite of his troubled past. He chose to spend time with people in his church. He listened to his pastor and to me. He listened to those with whom he worked in the ministry. He heeded godly wisdom and that made the crucial difference in his life. Ask yourself which you would rather be: the one who chose God's path or the one who chose his own.

Yes, Miguel experienced God's forgiveness. Yes, he experienced miracles. Yes, he had a change of heart. However, many people experience a change of heart yet never overcome their obstacles. Many people become good, yet never seem to break free from the chains holding them back. They never gain victory in their battles. They never break the barriers. They seem to be forever caught in the same frustrating patterns. Why? Because they lack a godly heart combined with godly wisdom.

Based upon the principles of God's wisdom, Miguel began to construct a life of healthy and decent principles that led him to break barriers few people in his hometown have ever been able to overcome. He began to make wise choices based upon wisdom learned from godly people.

Today, he and his family are actively pursuing God's plan for their lives. They have partnered with the Lord to break the patterns of self-destruction and the barriers that kept them in bondage.

Their victory is due to the wise choices they have made. Miguel's father continues to attend AA meetings. His mother continues to attend church and raise her kids in the wisdom of the Lord. Miguel continues to spend time with those who display godly wisdom. The old proverb is true: Birds of a feather flock together.

Surround yourself with people who are wise. Choose godly friends who will encourage you to be wise and make godly decisions.

## THE PROVERBS

The second practice for gaining the wisdom of Christ is from its written source, the Bible. The Proverbs of the Old Testament are one of the finest sources of godly wisdom we have. King Solomon wrote the book of Proverbs, and he is considered one of the wisest men in history.

Soon after he inherited the throne from his father, Solomon received a special proposal from God. God offered him whatever his heart desired. It was a onetime offer. Notice how Solomon responded to the Lord. Instead of responding to the Lord's offer with a laundry list of riches, glory, fame, and possessions, Solomon said, "Yes, give me wisdom and knowledge as I come and go among this people—for who on his own is capable of leading these, your glorious people?" (2 Chronicles 1:10 *The Message*). Imagine that! Of all the things Solomon could have asked the Lord to grant him, he asked for wisdom. Most people would have asked the Lord for at least half riches.

The Lord, impressed with Solomon's response, said, "Because of this, you get what you asked for—wisdom and knowledge. And I'm presenting you the rest as a bonus—money, wealth, and fame beyond anything the kings before or after you had or will have" (2 Chronicles 1:12 *The Message*).

Solomon was the son of King David. His mother was Bathsheba. He was raised in the palace, where he was accustomed to riches, political power, and fame. Once he became king, he had the opportunity to acquire whatever his heart desired. Everything was at his command and disposal. Further, God offered him something extraordinary. He could have been the richest and most powerful man in all of history.

By choosing not to ask the Lord for any of those things, he proved he was worthy of managing all of them. Instead of saying, "God, give me greatness," he said, "Give me wisdom and knowledge." His prayer reflected the old proverb that says, "Give a man a fish and feed him for a day. Teach a man to fish and feed him for the rest of his life." Instead of praying, "Lord, help me break one barrier today," he prayed, "Lord, teach me to break every barrier for the rest of my life."

Solomon's request was brilliant. He knew if he asked the Lord for wisdom and knowledge, all those other issues such as wealth, respect, health, and security would fall into place.

## THE PERFECT PRESCRIPTION

If I were a doctor, I would prescribe you a healthy dose of godly wisdom each day. Since I'm not a doctor, I encourage you to take the time to study the Bible, and specifically the book of Proverbs, every day. It is packed full of godly wisdom and values. It will give you the keys to unlock the door to godly knowledge, living, insights, perspective, and wisdom. It will give you the necessary tools to break any barrier, overcome adversity, and reach your greatest potential. In short, your ability to break barriers will become much more efficient and profitable as you gain God's perspective through wisdom.

There are thirty-one chapters in the book of Proverbs, one for each day of the month. On a sheet of paper, write down the highlights you pick up as you read through each chapter. Spend ten minutes a day studying each chapter. After the first week, add a chapter of the Psalms. After another week, add three chapters of any other book in the Bible, and continue to read through the book until you finish it. In doing this, you will read a total of five chapters a day (one from Proverbs, one from Psalms, and three chapters from another book). Your total reading time shouldn't be longer than thirty minutes.

It may not seem much at first. However, studying the Bible at this pace will allow you to read the book of Proverbs each month and the book of Psalms twice a year, as well as the entire Bible.

After one month you will notice a significant difference in your perspective and ability to confront the issues in your life. You will realize there is a noteworthy distinction between who you were prior to beginning the program and who you are now. After six months, the difference will be greater. After one year, the difference will be as night and day.

Once you have established a healthy habit of reading God's Word and growing in God's wisdom, feel free to add CDs or other books that pertain to the specific challenges you are facing, such as finances, health, family, or relationships. God will help you gain perspective as you study His Word, and He will help you with the specific barriers you need to overcome. Use the values outlined in Proverbs as the standard by which you judge all other forms of influence and guidance. Always remember the importance of using the Word as a baseline for values, ethics, and godly insight.

For example, if you want to break an insurmountable financial barrier, do not pick a get-rich-quick book to solve your money problems. That would be in direct opposition to the advice we find in Proverbs. Find guidance congruent with the values outlined in the Bible. As a rule, I always use the Bible as a benchmark for the values I embrace to help me break the barriers I face.

## FIVE SIMPLE WAYS TO BECOME WISE

Throughout the Bible, there are great lessons about how to become wise. God placed them there so you and I can live meaningful and significant lives. If we live our lives according to their guidance, we will inevitably overcome the barriers that keep us from reaching our greatest potential. Listed on the following pages are five simple ways to become wise.

## 1. Fear the Lord

As I mentioned earlier in this chapter, "The fear of the LORD is the beginning of wisdom" (Psalm 111:10 NIV). This concept is so important in establishing the second pillar that it's worth revisiting. In Proverbs 1, Solomon argues that in order to attain wisdom for understanding and living a prudent life, we must fear the Lord. Solomon understood the fear factor as a precursor to developing godly wisdom. Those who fear the Lord respect His direction and guidance. They heed His advice. And because of that respect, they are not caught up in the countless meaningless and unnecessary detours of life. They are not distracted by the temptations that would lure them away from wisdom and keep them from breaking barriers. Instead, they follow the advice and guidelines set forth by God, because they fearfully respect Him.

Sometimes, godly wisdom flies in the face of conventional wisdom. Of all the sons of Jesse, the Lord picked the smallest, youngest, and least likely to be king over Israel. David didn't stand out in a crowd. He didn't impress everyone with his stature. One thing is certain. He feared the Lord (see 1 Chronicles 16:25; 1 Samuel 26:7–11). And because of that, God chose him to be king.

If you fear the Lord, you'll be connected to God's wisdom, the fruit of which will help you live a life full of righteousness, justice, and fairness. To put it simply, you will be blessed! Fools, on the other hand, have no respect for God. Instead, they become caught in the clutches of sinful patterns of self-destruction, and they entice others to fall away from goodness and healthy living.

The Lord promises that if you display a healthy respect for Him, His wisdom and blessings will follow you all the days of your life and even unto your children's children (see Psalm 128:1–6)!

## 2. Don't Be Prideful

I like the way *The Message* spells it out: "First pride, then the crash—the bigger the ego, the harder the fall" (Proverbs 16:18). Pride is probably the single largest factor that prevents people from breaking their barriers. Generally speaking, people are stubborn and do not like correction. That's precisely the reason they are stuck where they are. Simply put, pride prevents people from getting out of their own way.

I have a good friend who pastors one of the largest churches in Central America. He has a special proverb for all the prideful, self-important people who refuse to listen to godly counsel. He says: "Pride is like bad breath. Everyone knows you have it, except you."

In response to people's stubbornness and pride, Solomon wrote: "If you had responded to my rebuke, I would have poured out my heart to you and made my thoughts known to you. But since you rejected me when I called and no one gave heed when I stretched out my hand, since you ignored all my advice and would not accept my rebuke, I in turn will laugh at your disaster; I will mock you when calamity overtakes you" (Proverbs 1:23–26 NIV). The Lord's wisdom would have come to their rescue had it not been for their pride.

If you desire to break barriers and become all that God has destined you to be, let go of your pride. Don't hold on to it. It blinds you and keeps you right where you are. Pride is the antithesis of the second pillar.

## 3. Obey Those in Authority

When you submit to those in authority and obey the laws of the land, you avoid paying fines and penalties, receiving reprimands and rebukes, and getting thrown into jail. Wise people know that the law functions to protect us from harm and pain. Those who serve in authority do so for our benefit. When we heed their guidance, we spare ourselves the grief and frustration of paying the price for breaking the law.

Some people argue that many in authority are corrupt and evil. That may be the case. There are examples throughout history of abuse of power. However, Paul lived in a society full of corruption, yet he strongly asserts in the Bible that "everyone must submit himself to the governing authorities, for there is no authority except that which God has established" (Romans 13:1 NIV).

My travels have taken me to a handful of countries where governments keep a very close eye on their people. It's fair to say that they rule with an iron fist. I've learned that if I behave, the door will always be open for me to return. If I obey the rulers and those in authority, the chances are very high that I won't find myself in a holding tank—even in countries where the government is corrupt. On the other hand, I've seen people who think they are above the system. They live life without any regard for the law or those in authority. Sooner or later, they reap what they have sown and pay a steep price for their arrogance.

Imagine the kind of world we would live in if everyone obeyed the laws of the land and the authorities who serve over them. How would that impact the number of accidents on our roads? How would that affect the percentage of children who become addicted to drugs? How many lives would be spared from violent crimes?

According to Paul, when we obey those in authority, our lives will be blessed. We will gain grace and favor. We will overcome life's challenges.

## 4. Commit to Reading and Studying Scripture

In elementary school, I couldn't read very well. I was consistently behind the rest of the class. Finally, my teacher sent me to "reading lab," a bungalow filled with sophisticated equipment to help students improve their reading skills. Every Wednesday, this eight-year-old boy humbly headed to the provisional classroom and spent forty-five painful minutes staring at moving words on a teleprompter. Have you ever felt scholastically challenged? I did, every Wednesday.

When I turned fifteen, I committed my life to Christ. Coming from a highly dysfunctional home, I had a new lease on life. But I still had plenty of barriers and challenges, not to mention a ton of baggage. I needed God to help me overcome many things in my life. That's when a friend in my youth group challenged me. He said, "If you want to see God change you and do great things in you, you must read His Word! Commit yourself to studying the Scriptures."

So I did. I bought a modern-day translation of the Bible and started to read several chapters a day. I discovered the richness of the Old Testament, the nuances of Paul's theology, and the power of a God who loved me and wanted to set me free.

After four months, I noticed that I was reading much faster, covering more material in a shorter amount of time, and reading with greater comprehension. But something more important was happening in me. The barriers, challenges, and baggage I was carrying became manageable. God's Word gave me strength. It gave me direction. It gave me wisdom. Through reading and studying the Scriptures, I began to renew my mind and reformat the hard drive in my head. God's wisdom began to blossom in my young adolescent heart.

Reading and studying Scripture will cement the second pillar in your life. Notice what the Bible says about the importance of God's Word: "Every part of Scripture is God-breathed and useful one way or another—showing us truth, exposing our rebellion, correcting our mistakes, training us to live God's way. Through the Word we are put together and shaped up for the tasks God has for us" (2 Timothy 3:16 *The Message*). Studying God's Word reaps a life full of blessing and wisdom.

## 5. Trust the Lord with All Your Heart

Trusting the Lord implies that we have faith in Him. We recognize that He can guide our lives better than we can. We yield our will and turn the reins of our hearts over to Him.

If there is one Scripture verse that sums up the second pillar, it's this one: "Trust in the LORD with all your heart and lean not on your own understanding" (Proverbs 3:5 NIV).

Acts 8:26–39 tells a powerful story about a man named Philip. He was being used in a powerful revival, when, suddenly, an angel of the Lord appeared to him and said, "Go south to the road—the desert road—that goes down from Jerusalem to Gaza" (verse 26 NIV). He never questioned why he should leave the city, a place that was experiencing many miracles. He never asked, "Why me?" He trusted the Lord and didn't try to figure things out on his own.

Sitting by the side of the road, he saw a chariot with an Ethiopian eunuch inside reading the scroll of the prophet Isaiah. The Spirit told him, "Go to that chariot and stay near it" (8:29 NIV). Again, he didn't question the Lord's leading. He didn't say, "What in the world are You asking of me? Are You sure You know what You're doing?"

Philip walked over to the chariot and asked the eunuch if he knew what he was reading. The eunuch replied, "How can I, unless someone explains it to me?" (8:31 NIV). The eunuch was an important man, in charge of all the treasury of Candace, queen of the Ethiopians. Philip climbed into the chariot and explained the Scripture and "told him the good news about Jesus" (verse 35 NIV). Philip baptized the eunuch, and suddenly the Spirit of the Lord took Philip away. The eunuch returned home and proclaimed the gospel message to his country.

Sometimes we simply need to trust the Lord and lean not on our own understanding. Sometimes we need to let go and let God take over. Philip could have said, "Uh, what's Your game plan, Lord? This doesn't sound logical to me." Instead, he trusted the Lord, and as a result, an entire nation was reached.

When you feel that barriers are mounting all around, when you feel as if there is no hope for tomorrow, when you think you've used up all your options, when nothing makes sense, trust the Lord and lean not on your own understanding. He will be there for you. God will help you, because He loves you. That is one of the wisest things you can do.

Imagine having the wisdom to know the right time to quit your job and start a new career. Wouldn't it be great to know when to buy or sell your home or make changes to your retirement portfolio? Imagine having the godly wisdom to choose the right mate before you commit to spending the rest of your life with that person. Wouldn't you like to have God's perspective to know how many kids you should have and when? Imagine how radically different your life will be as you embrace the wisdom of Christ. Putting these five lessons into practice will serve you well in your quest to be wise and godly.

⌒◈⌒

Godly wisdom is a step above all other forms of common sense and wisdom. It is the ability to make decisions based upon God's perspective. In essence, it is the ability to see the world from a heavenly perspective. Because of God's omnipotence and omnipresence, He can see the world from every angle. This is what distinguishes the wisdom of God from common sense. As we partner with Him, we gain His insights into how to overcome the adversities we face.

The starting point for gaining godly wisdom is found in Psalm 111: "The fear of the LORD is the beginning of wisdom; all who follow his precepts have good understanding" (verse 10 NIV). As we render unto the Lord respect, we open ourselves to His guidance, teaching, and insights. We gain godly wisdom by first surrounding ourselves with people who have it. Then we study the Proverbs every day.

In the next chapter, we will focus on practical ways to unleash the power of Christ's wisdom in our life. Undoubtedly, as we continue to partner with God and seek His wisdom, He will give us all that is necessary to overcome the challenges we face.

As we close out this chapter, let's ask the Lord for His divine direction and guidance to help us break the barriers we face. Once again, I ask you to join me in a simple prayer asking God to help us grasp new innovative perspectives to become all we are destined to be:

*Lord, I realize You are omnipotent and omnipresent and Your perspective is infinite. You are the Creator of the heavens and the earth. You are all-powerful, the Almighty, the Beginning and the End.*

*Forgive me for the pride I have displayed and for my refusal to seek your guidance. I do not want to be a prideful person. I do not want to stay stuck in my destructive patterns. I want to be free—free to live out the great potential You have destined for me.*

*I do not ask You for riches, glory, fame, or political power. I ask You for wisdom. Help me to become a person with a godly heart, filled with the wisdom of Christ.*

*I recognize I cannot break barriers alone. I need Your help. I need Your wisdom. Give me Your insights, Your perspective, and Your understanding. Help my respect for You to grow every day. Give me the strength to read Your Word and absorb Your heart and Your wisdom. In Christ's name I pray. Amen.*

# CHAPTER 5

# Unleashing the Power of Christ's Wisdom in Your Life

JOHN 8:2–11 illustrates the power of Christ's wisdom. Early in the morning, the crowds gathered in the temple courts anxiously awaiting Jesus' arrival. There was an air of expectancy for something wonderful. When Jesus appeared, the crowds hushed as He sat down in the chair and began to teach. All of a sudden, the Pharisees interrupted the meeting and brought forward a woman who had been caught in adultery. Forcing her to stand in front of everyone, they turned to Jesus and said, "Teacher, this woman was caught in the act of adultery. In the Law Moses commanded us to stone such women. Now what do you say?" (verses 4–5 NIV).

The question was a setup. They were looking for a way to accuse Him. Instead of taking the bait, He stooped down and began to write something on the ground with His finger.

"Come on!" they insisted. "We need an answer. Don't you know what the Law commands us to do?" Finally, He stood, looked sternly into their eyes, and said, "If any one of you is without sin, let him be the first to throw a stone at her" (8:7 NIV). They had no reply. They could say nothing.

With that, He bent down and began to write again.

One by one, the Pharisees began to disburse. At first the older ones left, until they had all gone. Finally only two people remained where the crowd once stood. Jesus got up and said to the woman, "Woman, where are [the people who are accusing you]? Has no one condemned you?" (8:10 NIV).

"No one, sir," she said (8:11 NIV).

Jesus said, "Then neither do I condemn you. Go now and leave your life of sin" (8:11 NIV).

Every time I read this passage, I ask the same question: How do you catch a woman in adultery without catching a man? Shouldn't there have been a woman *and* a man standing before Jesus? The fact that only the woman was present implies that it was a trap from the start. Clearly the teachers of the law and the Pharisees gave the man a way out. That is, if there truly *was* an adulterous encounter. Since they were demanding capital punishment for someone who was set up, it became very obvious that the person on trial was not the woman but Jesus.

Once they continued to press Him for an answer, He delivered the knockout blow. His statement was not simply referring to the general idea that we all have sin in our lives and fall short of God's glory and therefore have no right to punish those caught in crime. If that were the case, no judicial system could stand. No prosecutor, police officer, defense attorney, public official, or judge is without sin. Instead, Jesus was referring to how they had entrapped her and maliciously brought her to trial. He discerned this and then invited them to kill her—provided they could prove they were blameless in the process. In essence, He was calling their bogus trial sinful.

They were caught, and they knew it. Today, this is called malicious prosecution. The older ones knew what they had done and began to leave until, finally, no one was left.

Was the woman innocent? Probably not. Jesus never denied their accusations against her. After He turned the tables on them, He did not let her off the hook. He ended His encounter with her by saying: "Go now and leave your life of sin" (8:11 NIV).

Have you ever felt backed into a corner with no way out? Have you ever felt surrounded, with no solution in sight? Have you ever felt that your barriers were insurmountable, impassable, or impenetrable? Throughout the four Gospels, Jesus was surrounded dozens of times, yet He demonstrated the power of God's wisdom. When the world around you seems to be coming apart at the seams, when the chips are down and there's no hope in sight, when it looks like you have no way out, the wisdom of Christ can guide you to the solution. It's the wisdom of Christ that makes the difference.

Remember, being good isn't good enough! Being a nice, law-abiding citizen can only take you so far. Without His wisdom, you'll never make the quantum leap you yearn to make. You'll never make the jump to the next level. You'll never break the barrier that separates you from all you're destined to become.

Choose God's wisdom for your life, and your possibilities will be endless. Your potential will have no limits. God will lead you from survival mode to a life that thrives! Unleash the power of Christ's wisdom in your life, and the challenges you face will become surmountable.

In the previous chapter, we began the process of establishing the second pillar in our lives, that is, godly wisdom. We discovered the importance of seeing things from God's perspective. We also looked at five simple ways to become wise and the importance of studying the Proverbs and gleaning wisdom from those around you.

This chapter focuses on unleashing the power of Christ's wisdom in our lives. We will discover some practical ways the wisdom of God can break the barriers we face. When you complete this chapter, the second pillar will be in place.

## DANIEL AND SOLOMON

There was a very popular story that circulated throughout the land of Israel two thousand years ago. Although it originated sometime around 400 BC, everyone during the time of Christ would have heard it. Although this story is not found in the Old Testament, it demonstrates the justice and wisdom of God in a compelling way. The following is paraphrased from the book of Daniel and Susanna found in the Revised Standard Version.

Susanna was a beautiful woman whose stunning appearance was surpassed only by her fear of the Lord. She guarded the laws of God in her heart, because her father, Hilkiah, made sure she was raised in the teachings of Jewish tradition. Both of her parents were righteous people. One day a man named Joakim went to them and asked for their daughter's hand in marriage. They kindly agreed.

He was a very rich man and had a large estate with a spacious garden. All the Jews in the area would come to visit, because he was the most admired man in the community.

That same year, two elders became judges to govern the people. But the condition of their hearts caused the Lord to grieve. He said, "They are filled with iniquity." These two judges often went to Joakim's house because many people who had civil problems and lawsuits gathered there every morning.

Each day, when everyone went home for lunch, Susanna enjoyed an afternoon stroll in her garden. As the two elders observed her, day after day, walking through the garden, they began to desire her. Because of their lust, their minds became twisted. They lost their sound judgment and failed to follow the laws of God.

Each day, like a lion stalking its prey, they eagerly watched her. On one occasion, while everyone else was gone, each elder noticed that the other hadn't left. When they pressed each other, they eventually confessed their lustful desire to be with her. So they began to devise a plan for when they could find her alone without her husband.

Finally, the day came when she went into the garden with only two attendants. It was a hot day, and she wanted to bathe and cool herself from the scorching sun. Everyone else went home for lunch except the two elders. That's when they decided to make their move. They hid themselves in the back of the garden and watched her from a distance.

Susanna turned to her two maids and said, "Please bring me some oil and ointments. After you bring them to me, leave the garden and shut the garden gates behind you so I can bathe." Her maids did exactly as she instructed them and shut the garden gates behind them. They did not see the two elders lurking behind the bushes, because they had hid themselves.

When the maids left, the two elders, their hearts filled with lust, rushed toward her and said, "Everyone has left. The garden gates are closed. We cannot see out, nor can anyone see in. We are in love with you, and if you agree, we want you to lie with us. If you deny us this, we will publicly testify that we saw you lying with a young man and that was the reason you told your maids to leave."

Susanna's heart sank. In utter dismay she said, "There is no way out. If I do such a thing, I will be put to death for adultery and for sinning against the Lord. If I do not, you will surely bring the judgment of my entire house and community against me. I will not be able to escape your hands. So I choose not to commit such a horrific act and fall into your lustful plan."

Then Susanna cried in a loud voice and the two elders shouted even louder, creating a disturbance in the middle of the garden. When the household servants heard the screaming coming from the garden, they ran toward the commotion. One of the elders ran and opened the gates. Then the elders told the servants their tale. Nothing like that had ever been said about Susanna, and the servants felt ashamed.

The following day, the elders came to the house of Joakim with wickedness in their hearts. They never deviated from their evil plot to have Susanna put to death. They sent for her, saying, "Bring us Susanna, the daughter of Hilkiah, who is the wife of Joakim." She entered with her children, her parents, and her entire family.

Being a beautiful woman of great refinement, to the elders' dismay, she came in hidden behind a veil. The wicked men, filled with lust, wanted to see her beauty one last time. So they ordered that her veil be removed. Her friends, family, and all who knew her watched as the veil was removed, and they wept.

As Susanna stood in tears before the assembly, the two elders stood in the midst of the crowd, placed their evil hands upon her head, and said, "Yesterday we were in the garden alone. This woman came in with two servants, shut the doors, and dismissed them. A young man who was hiding came to her and lay with her. When we saw this wickedness, our hearts fell. We ran to them, but the young man overpowered us, opened the gates, and escaped.

When we questioned her as to who the young man was, she refused to tell us. We seized her and brought her to this trial. These things we testify."

Because the elders held honorable positions, the crowd believed them. So they condemned her to death.

Susanna raised her voice and said, "O eternal God, You know what is secret, and You are aware of all the wicked things these men have invented against me!"

The Lord heard her cry.

God shook the conscience of a young man named Daniel just as they were leading her away to be put to death. With a loud voice he said, "I am innocent of the blood of this woman." Everyone in the assembly turned to him and asked, "What did you say?" With confidence and self-assurance he answered, "Are you so blind that you cannot see that you have been lied to, you sons of Israel? Are you so ready to condemn a daughter of Israel without looking at all the facts? These men have deceived us all. I ask that we return to the place of judgment."

The assembly returned to order. The elders, in their arrogance, said to him, "Come and sit with us. You have every right to show us her innocence."

Then Daniel said to the assembly, "Separate these two elders far from each other, and I will examine each of them."

The crowd separated them, and Daniel began his interrogation. He called the first one in and said, "You are wicked, and now your sins have returned to reveal your evil heart. You have given false judgments. You've condemned the innocent and let the guilty go free. You've done all this even though the Lord said not to condemn a righteous person. Tell me the truth, if you really saw her, under which tree did you see them together?"

The elder replied, "Under the mastic tree."

Then Daniel said, "You have lied against yourself. For the Lord's angel has received your death sentence and is coming to cut you in two!"

He gave orders to put him aside. Then they brought in the other elder. Daniel turned to him and said, "You are not an offspring of Judah. Beauty has deceived your heart and you are filled with lust. You have been chasing the daughters of Israel, and they were intimate with you because of fear, but this daughter did not endure your wickedness. Tell me, under which tree did you catch the couple being intimate?"

The elder replied, "Under an evergreen oak."

Then Daniel said, "Very well! You too are a liar. The Lord's angel is waiting with sword in hand to cut you in two. He will destroy you both."

The entire assembly shouted with joy, "God saves those who place their trust in Him." Then they seized the two wicked elders who lied against Susanna, and they did to them what they had planned to do to her. Acting in accordance with the law of Moses, the assembly put them to death. Innocent blood was saved that day, and Susanna's mother and father and family praised God, because there was nothing shameful found in her.

In Daniel's cross-examination, he brilliantly exposed the elders' evil hearts by asking them one question they never anticipated. A mastic tree is commonly considered a shrub and can only grow up to twelve feet in height, while the evergreen oak in its majestic stature can reach over fifty feet tall. Upon hearing their answers, the people knew they were liars. The two elders condemned themselves by their own words.

Daniel unleashed the power of God's wisdom. In doing so, he saved a young woman's life, restored her reputation, and brought two wicked men to justice. As you face those who would seek your demise, remember that God's wisdom is your trump card. No challenge, burden, or barrier is a match for the power of God's wisdom. So unleash it. Doing so is the *wisest* thing you can do!

Daniel understood the need to have God's insight and perspective to make good decisions. He recognized that God provides the wisdom we need to break barriers, overcome adversity, and reach our greatest potential.

Daniel wasn't the only one who understood this. Solomon did as well. Without God's perspective, Solomon would have never become the wise ruler he was. First Kings 3:16–28 tells the story of two angry prostitutes living in the same house who had a fierce quarrel and brought their case before Solomon.

The first one said, "Each of us had a baby three days apart. While the house was empty, this woman's baby died during the night. Then she got up and switched her dead baby for mine. When I woke up to nurse mine, he was dead! When I looked closely, I discovered that he wasn't my child." Then the other woman raised her voice and said, "That's not true! My son is the one that's alive." And they argued back and forth until finally Solomon said, "You two keep arguing back and forth claiming the child is yours. This one says this. The other one says that. So I'll tell you what. I'll have him cut in two pieces. That way you can each take half the baby home with you."

The woman whose son was alive couldn't stand the thought of her baby being cut in two. So she cried out and said, "Please, my lord, give her the living baby! Don't kill him!" But the other one said, "The king's solution sounds good to me. Cut him in two! If I can't have him neither shall you!"

That's when Solomon's wisdom was revealed. He said, "Give the baby to the first woman. She's the rightful mother." When the people heard the king's verdict, they were all in awe because they knew that his wisdom had come from God.

Solomon unleashed the wisdom of God and saved a life and a family. That's the type of wisdom God wants to impart to you. He wants you to take on new ways of seeing the world around you. He wants you to see the world from His perspective. He wants to give you new paradigms and perspectives. No matter the predicament, no matter the challenge, no matter the circumstances you are facing, when you unleash the power of God's wisdom, the playing field is changed forever.

## NEW PARADIGMS AND PERSPECTIVES

Many times, the answers we seek are right before our eyes. It's like looking for house keys that are in your hand the entire time. You frantically search your purse or pockets, briefcase, desk, vehicle, and kitchen countertop, along with ten other locations. Then your spouse says, "What are those in your hand?"

And you say to yourself *If my keys were a snake, it would have bitten me.* What prevented you from seeing the keys?

The lenses through which we see the world prevent us from seeing things from different angles. Our perspective sometimes prevents us from seeing the most important and obvious choice. To change this, we need a new paradigm. To see the way around the barriers we face, we need a fresh point of view. We need to see our circumstances from God's position.

When I was seventeen, I decided to attend Vanguard University to prepare myself for full-time ministry. My heart was set on becoming a minister. My parents were not enthusiastic about the idea. They feared that after graduation I would not be able to survive the financial pressures of life. My dad said to me, "Son, just remember, if you go into ministry, you won't be making a lot of money." Looking back, I can honestly say he was right.

I think my parents would have been more encouraging if I had chosen a secular university. Although they were supportive of my religious convictions, they were concerned about whether I could afford to live in California while working as a minister. For a few weeks, we were at odds, and there was an uncomfortable tension between us.

One day, my father was working in his bar, and a regular customer of the restaurant walked in. His name was Chick Hearn, the radio announcer for the Los Angeles Lakers for more than four decades. He had moved from Minnesota with the Lakers when they set up shop in Los Angeles. Many people consider Chick to be one of the finest announcers the game has ever had. I know the people from L.A. definitely think so.

Chick came into my dad's bar and waited for a table in the dining room. He normally had a cup of coffee while the two conversed about life and the Lakers.

That afternoon, Chick detected that my dad was a bit distracted. He said, "What seems to be troubling you, Bobby?"

My dad replied, "It's my son. He wants to go to a religious college to prepare for ministry. My only concern is that he won't be able to pay the bills of life. I am not sure what to do."

Chick put his coffee cup down on the bar and looked my father square in the eye. After pausing for a brief second he said, "Well, I lost someone very dear to me to a drug overdose. If I could rewind the tapes of his life and see him through ministry school, I would do it in a heartbeat."

Chick saw things from a heavenly perspective. He saw things from an eternal viewpoint. His painful experience gave him a unique insight into the wisdom of God. He could approach the issue with godly wisdom. And to my father's credit, he had enough common sense to see things from this point of view as well. This one comment tipped the scales in favor of my father supporting my efforts to go to college and prepare for ministry.

In a moment, my father had a paradigm shift. His perception and interpretation of the priorities of life changed. During my four years of college, he carried most of the financial burden. Several weeks each year, he worked sixteen hours a day to cover the cost of my tuition. I am grateful to him for his efforts. I am thankful for his support to help me through college. I am even more impressed, however, by his willingness to consider the world from a different perspective.

So much of what we think and how we approach our barriers is determined by our point of view. It's determined by our mindset. One of the wisest things we can do as we attempt to break the barriers is allow Christ's wisdom to change our perspective.

In our quest to break barriers, it is imperative to reach beyond our normal perspective. We need to grow in God's wisdom and allow Him to change our point of view about our circumstances. Any barrier can be approached from different angles. We must be careful not to think the way we see the world is the only way to see it.

## FIVE STEPS FOR BREAKING BARRIERS USING WISE JUDGMENT

Knowing my heart is aligned with the character of God, when I face a barrier, I first pursue His wisdom. I sit down and imagine the barrier having some sort of physical form. Then I visualize our confrontation. I face the barrier head-on. Running from my problems is not an option. Hiding isn't an alternative. I must face the music. I lay out five specific steps I know I must complete in order to see my barrier or obstacle overcome. As I share these five necessary steps, write down some of the ideas that come to your mind to coincide with these steps. Without a doubt, they will help you in your journey to break your barriers.

## 1. Begin with Prayer

Before we attempt to break through whatever is preventing us from overcoming adversity, we must pray. Connecting with God is the starting point for everything we do. Ask the Lord for His insight and wisdom to negotiate the problem. Ask Him to allow you to see the barrier from His perspective. Seeing the barrier from God's point of view will allow you to visualize not only the barrier's strengths but also its weaknesses.

My wife, Cindee, and I wanted to purchase a house but had very little money. We had no equity and had never owned property before. Given the high cost of real estate in California, the odds of our purchasing a house were less than we hoped. We believed it was time for us to make a purchase and felt God would open the right doors. So we prayed. That was our starting point. We asked the Lord to open our minds to the possibilities beyond our own limited perspective. We felt peace and sensed our motives were right, and thus we could continue in the process.

## 2. Reexamine the Barrier

After praying, we moved on to the next step. We reexamined the barrier from every possible angle. Instead of looking at the overwhelming circumstances of a real-estate market constantly appreciating and moving beyond our financial capabilities, we broke the barrier down into smaller parts. Instead of facing the problem from one particular angle, we decided to get a different perspective. I liken it to flying around a mountain in a helicopter, circling several times. Figuratively speaking, this enabled us to see the problem from every angle and gain a different outlook on our barrier. It also allowed us to break the problem down into smaller parts. As a result, we could see both the strong and the weak points of the barrier that stood in our way.

Every barrier, no matter how large, can be broken down into smaller parts. Buying a house entails many details. Besides finding a desirable house, you also need a down payment. Qualifying for the right loan and being able to make the monthly payments are no small accomplishments. Of course, escrow involves many fine points as well.

Cindee and I, along with our Realtor, broke the barrier of buying a home into smaller segments and addressed each one independently. We took it one day at a time, one obstacle at a time. If we had thought we needed to come up with the funds for a down payment and monthly payments all in one day, we would have given up. If we would have had to find a decent home close to good schools for our girls and manage all the details of escrow all in one day, we would have been overwhelmed. We would have quit.

We realized something about California real estate. People just like us buy property in California—they find ways to break the barrier. It's not an impenetrable fortress. It can be done. As we broke the barrier down into smaller segments, we began to discover its weaknesses. For instance, there are sellers who are anxious to move and sell their property for less than it is worth. Lower interest rates reduce the monthly payments of those who have large mortgages. It has never been easier to build a home. Depending on one's perspective, prices are low compared to what they will be in twenty years when California's population swells from a little over thirty-three million to forty-six million (see the U.S. Census Bureau's newsroom: http://www.census.gov/Press-Release/www/releases/archives/population/004704.html). We began to see cracks in the seeming impenetrable barrier, and we knew those cracks might allow us to reach our goal.

## 3. Embrace Every Possible Solution

We looked at and wrote down every possible solution imaginable. We looked at attached condos, detached condos, detached homes, townhomes, and new homes under construction. We wrote down the name of every family member from whom we thought we could borrow money to help with the down payment. We analyzed our projected income and looked at our retirement and savings accounts. Further, we did an inventory of everything we owned and appraised it for the purposes of converting it into cash. We consulted three different mortgage brokers and told them all they would be bidding against the others for our loan. We asked them about every possible loan and considered the amount our monthly payments would be based on a 20 percent, 10 percent, and 5 percent down payment. Suddenly the creative wisdom of God began to formulate some very interesting ideas in our minds.

As you creatively face your barrier, write down every possible solution that comes to mind. No answer, no solution, is ridiculous. Every idea you put down on paper is worthy of acknowledging. Do not erase or discount any idea no matter how ridiculous it may sound. Once you have written down every idea and feel positive about your list, you will be able to move on to the fourth step.

## 4. Analyze Your Top Five Choices, and Draw Up Follow-Through Strategies

After compiling a list of every possible solution, begin to reduce it to the top five. Then, for each one, construct a chronological or sequential plan with the necessary steps to carry it through to its logical conclusion. This will allow you to see the strengths and weaknesses of each idea. For us, this was especially helpful when we were analyzing different loan options and interest rates. Lenders vary from state to state and country to country. There have never been as many options for loans as there are today. If we hadn't looked at each option independently and mapped it out to its conclusion, we might have chosen one we would have regretted.

A friend of mine, Don Judkins, once told me, "No matter what solution you choose for a problem, always have a way out. Make sure you can get out of your commitment in case of necessity. Always have an exit strategy." This is great advice from someone who has worked in real estate his entire life. For every solution, no matter how good it may seem, there must be a tangible and decent exit strategy. If something happens to your health or something prevents you from moving forward, know your way out. Always have a plan B and a plan C. Once we made our choice on the home, loan, down payment amount, and offer, we moved on to the fifth step.

## 5. Continue to Seek Godly Advice from Wise People

During the entire process, Cindee and I continued soliciting input from those who had walked this road before.

Cindee and I had done all of our homework. We prayed. We reexamined the barrier and broke it into smaller segments. We embraced every possible solution. We analyzed the top five solutions and kept consulting those around us. Finally, we were concerned that our monthly payments were going to be too high, given our down payment. We were not going to make the purchase, and we were very disappointed. After several weeks of searching for a home, researching loans, and calculating our budgets, we were greatly saddened. Just before we pulled the plug on our venture, we called our real-estate agent, who encouraged us to call a mutual friend who had accomplished what we were trying to do.

Our friend and his family are missionaries who served in Central America for many years and managed to purchase a home in Southern California. I called him and explained our situation. He said, "Your issue is not a mortgage problem but a cash flow problem." Then, after he understood all our resources and dilemmas, he said, "Why not put down a little less than you originally planned? Your monthly payments will go up a bit. But you can use those funds as a cushion in case it's difficult to make the monthly payments. According to the budget you've laid out, the cushion will help supplement your monthly payments for three or four years, and maybe you'll never need to use it. By that time, the house will appreciate. It's worth the investment."

All of a sudden, the light went on. We saw things from a different perspective. The answer was as clear as day. That night Cindee and I went to bed knowing that, with our current salary, we could make our monthly mortgage payments for four years. Instead of paying rent into someone else's pocket, we would be investing in our future. Our friend had learned something through his struggles on a missionary's salary, and he shared it with us. We learned the importance of continuously asking for the input of those who had been down the road we desired to travel. To this day, we've never used the additional funds.

My greatest resources are the wise individuals around me. Your greatest resources are the wise people around you. Most likely, you have the individuals, knowledge, and information necessary at your disposal. Therefore, keep seeking the advice of those who have successfully overcome the same barrier or a barrier similar to the one you need to overcome. Ask them to give you insight, perspective, and an approach that is fitting for your situation. In most cases, they will be more than willing to help.

Before you begin, pray and ask for God's perspective. Then reexamine your barrier so you can see a clearer picture of it. Look at it from every angle and break it down into smaller segments. Think of every creative way through it. Analyze the top five results, and mentally carry them through to their logical conclusions. Finally, keep seeking godly advice from those who are wise.

Through it all, God will use your creativity and the creativity of those around you to help you plot a godly course to break the barriers you face. Here is a simple acronym to help you remember the steps I have outlined above. It spells BREAK:

1. **B**egin with prayer. Ask the Lord for wisdom to see things from His perspective.
2. **R**eexamine (research) the barrier. Look at it from every angle and break it down into smaller segments.
3. **E**mbrace every possible solution no matter how ridiculous it may sound.
4. **A**nalyze your top five results, and draw up a follow-through strategy for each one.
5. **K**eep seeking godly advice from wise people.

## REACHING AN ENTIRE NATION
## THROUGH GOD'S CREATIVITY

Recently, we were planning one of the largest outreaches in the history of our crusade ministry. It was to be held in the largest soccer stadium in Costa Rica. For the past seven years, our crusades have been divided into two segments. The children's segment begins at 5:30 p.m., and the youth/adult segment starts at 7:00 p.m. My wife and her staff coordinate a wonderful outreach that reaches thousands of children each night. I speak to the youth and adults.

We were looking for a way to reach out to thousands of children and invite them to the event. One morning, after my wife and I had spent our usual time together at our favorite Italian café, we drove by a McDonald's. An idea popped into my head. I thought, *Wouldn't it be great to put some sort of invitation into every Happy Meal to promote the children's portion of the crusade?*

PowerMark is a comic book series designed by Quest Ministries International. It presents the message of salvation and God's love in a way that children can easily understand. It is a first-rate piece of literature printed with the same quality as any Batman, Spider-Man, or Superman comic book. We decided to ask our denomination for several hundred thousand copies of the six-part series. Our strategy was to place a copy of volume one in every Happy Meal sold during the three months leading up to our event.

I made an appointment with the executives of McDonald's in Costa Rica. They took several samples and promised to bring it before their next board meeting. There was one small problem: their monthly Happy Meal sales at the time were not enough to cover the nation. We talked to other vendors as well, but no one was able to promise they could reach the number of children we wanted to reach.

We were caught in a difficult position. We wanted to reach the children of the nation, but how? We began to think about the means of distribution already in place. We asked ourselves, "Who has the power to distribute several hundred thousand pieces of literature in one single power shot?" Then the idea came to us: the largest and most powerful means of distribution in Costa Rica is the national newspaper. The largest national newspaper, which has close to three hundred thousand copies in circulation, is called *La Nación*. It is one of the most distinguished newspapers in Central America. We made an appointment and went in to talk with their executives.

They handed me a list showing their Sunday morning distribution. Hundreds of thousands of copies of the national newspaper are delivered every Sunday morning. This was the distribution we were looking for.

My ministerial associate Rebecca Ruiz spearheaded the negotiations. She said, "We need to place this piece of literature into the hands of every child in this country. We want to invite them to an event we are holding at the Saprissa soccer stadium. We believe the Lord loves the children of this country, and we want to share with them the love of God in a way that builds their self-esteem and dignity. And we need your help to do it. We want you to insert a copy of volume one of the series in the center of the Sunday morning paper the weekend before the event." Without hesitation, they agreed.

The comic book was the first volume in a six-volume series. It was an ongoing story line made up of six parts. In order to find out how the story developed and ended, all six parts were necessary. We received several hundred thousand copies of volume one, which was going to be distributed in the newspaper. Volumes two through five would be given out at the crusade. On the back of the comic books was a four-by-three-inch blank box that could be used for printing a customized message. We added a message with instructions on how to attend the crusade and obtain the rest of the series. The message read, "To find out the rest of this exciting story, come to the Saprissa soccer stadium and you will receive your free copy."

Each night, thousands of children stormed the gates of the stadium looking for their free copies of PowerMark. My wife gave a first-rate presentation of the gospel message, and several hundred children came forward for salvation each night. The response was overwhelming, to say the least. At the end of the children's crusade, we handed out a new volume of the comic book. After the fourth night of the crusade, children had received volumes one through five.

Finally, on the last night, we announced, "In order to receive your free copy of the last volume with its grand finale, go to one of these local churches." There was a list of local churches that had supported the event. In each church, every copy of the Power-Mark series was available. The following Sunday, thousands of children entered the doors of local churches all over Costa Rica. They found not only the final copy of the six-part series but a spiritual home as well.

God's creativity broke through a huge barrier. Children all over Costa Rica received the first volume of the comic book through a secular means of distribution. They were then guided to an evangelistic event where they found the love of Christ. Each night, they received the continuation of an intriguing children's story. They were then led to a local church where they received the final volume of the series and were given the chance to feel accepted, feel loved, and be discipled in the teachings of the Bible. The new idea worked better than any evangelistic literature outreach we had ever attempted. Tens of thousands of children were reached. Tens of thousands came to the crusade. Thousands had an encounter with Christ and are being discipled. To date, it is one of the greatest outreaches through literature distribution in the history of that country. We prayed, reexamined the barrier, and embraced every possible solution. Then we narrowed our ideas down to a few and kept consulting with those who had worked in distribution before. God's creativity touched an entire nation, and an insurmountable barrier was broken.

Two years later, the Luis Palau Evangelistic Association surpassed what we did by utilizing advertising spaces on the sides of buses and around bus terminals and held a crusade four times the size of ours. Praise God!

Thus far, we have discussed the importance of exploring new paradigms and ideas. We have talked about thinking outside the box and stretching our ability to see beyond that which lies immediately before us. We have also learned that we need to face our barriers head-on, praying through them, embracing every possible solution, and breaking them down into smaller sizes. In the remaining portion of this chapter, we will build an appreciation for an important skill that will help us be successful in our acquisition of godly wisdom: listening.

## BECOMING THE MOST INTERESTING PERSON IN THE ROOM

There is one easy way to become the most interesting person in the room: ask questions and listen. Listening is a skill very few people master. Most of us hear what we want to hear instead of what the other person wants to say. For this reason, there are huge communication gaps in many conversations. In order to reduce our never-ending miscommunications, we need to improve our listening skills. Doing so will help us in our quest for godly wisdom.

The doors of the elevator opened and a producer for a national morning television show stepped in. I thought, *Here I am in a New York City skyscraper, riding to the top floor in an elevator with a producer from a national network.* Unfortunately, I wasn't the only one heading up. The elevator was packed. Everyone scooted to the back and sides to give her room to join us.

As soon as she reached her spot and turned to face the closing doors, a famous literary agent standing in front of me gently touched her elbow and said, "Hey, Jen, how have you been?"

"Fine, thanks," she replied.

He continued, "If you have thirty seconds, I want to share something with you. I have a fantastic guest for your show!"

Little did I know I was about to witness a famous "elevator pitch."

She said, "Well, I get off on the eighteenth floor. So go for it!"

He said, "I have a phenomenal author who wrote a book. . . ." And he showed her the title.

She said, "Wow, that is a great title! Hey, I'm curious. Of these ten secrets listed on the cover, what's number one?"

He paused and said, "Uh, I don't know."

"What?!" she said. "What do you mean you don't know?"

"I can't remember," he said.

Clearly disappointed with his answer, she replied, "Well, obviously it didn't have that big of an impact on you. Besides, I would have liked to know what two and three are as well." With that, the doors of the elevator opened, and she walked out.

The agent didn't say a word as she made her exit. He had let a golden opportunity slip away. Had he simply asked the producer for a meeting at a later date, he could've given his author the chance of a lifetime and possibly changed his writing career forever! I'm quite certain the agent should have asked the producer for a one-on-one meeting so she could have asked the author all the questions she wanted. Given her demeanor, she would have agreed. Unfortunately, the agent didn't hear her, and he didn't use the opportunity to clarify her concerns.

Listening is a valuable trait, and it is necessary in order to increase one's wisdom. The verb *speak, spoke,* or *spoken* appears 654 times in the NIV Bible. The verbs for *listen, hear,* or *heard* are used more than 1,240 times. In the book of Proverbs alone, the mandate to listen appears sixteen times. God places a high priority on the ability to listen and heed advice. Someone once said, "God has given us one mouth and two ears. There is probably a good reason for the ratio."

If we are going to become wise people and grow in the wisdom of Christ, we must perfect our ability to listen and absorb the information wise individuals share with us. When entering a conversation, try to remember the following nuggets:

## 1. Hear What the Individual Is Trying to Say

Your commitment first and foremost should be to hear what the individual is trying to say. You should not be trying to hear only what you *want* the other person to say. This requires complete concentration, free from distractions and mental interruptions.

Married couples often struggle with this because at times husbands and wives are forced to communicate with each other in unfavorable circumstances. The phone is ringing. The kids are screaming. The dinner is burning. The bath is running. And unfortunately, many husbands and wives listen for what they want to hear instead of what the other person wants to communicate. As you begin a conversation, wipe the slate clean and rid yourself of all distractions and hidden motives.

## 2. Have Paper and Pen Handy

Keep a piece of paper and a pen handy to help you formulate questions as they come to your mind.

How many times have you heard someone say the following: "Uh, what was I going to say?" Then that statement is often followed with: "Oh, well. It must not have been important." Not true—the mind is constantly thinking ahead and solving problems. Sometimes, the very question we need answered is the one we have forgotten.

If you jot down a few words of your question or comment, your mind is freed to continue listening attentively to what your friend is sharing. Also, many of us are plagued by mental distractions when listening to others. I urge you to write down any of the chores or errands that come to mind. By writing down a couple of words that pertain to the distraction or unrelated task, your mind will be released to return to the discussion and remain actively engaged.

## 3. Give the Person Feedback

Tell the other person how you are receiving what they are trying to say. This gives him or her an opportunity to clarify if you have heard or understood something incorrectly. This also gives them a chance to reword something they are having a difficult time communicating. Every time they share a point, you can say something like, "May I ask you a question? Are you saying that . . . ?" You'll have much greater success doing it this way instead of responding, "You've got to be crazy!" or, "You can't be serious!" When the person who is sharing with you feels that you understand, he or she will be more inclined to share additional valuable information in the future.

Let's take a moment to consider what we have learned so far about breaking the barriers in our lives. A strong understanding of our purpose is the first requirement to break any barrier that stands before us. The next is a godly heart. Once we cultivate the heart of God within us, we need His wisdom. The wisdom of Christ gives us a godly perspective as we gain His insight, perspective, and ability to make sound decisions. God's perspective opens our eyes to new and creative ways to triumph over the adversity in our lives.

In this chapter, we've learned that as we approach a barrier, we should always begin with prayer. Prayer is the starting point for attaining God's perspective as we face obstacles. Then, we should reexamine the barrier, embrace every possible solution, analyze the best options, and seek godly advice from wise people.

Congratulations, the second pillar is now in place. You are one step closer to living the life God wants you to live!

The next two chapters focus on the role of the Holy Spirit, who gives us the strength and discipline to make good decisions based upon godly character. The Spirit gives us the power to complete the process of breaking our barriers and becoming all God has destined us to be.

As we close this chapter together, I am going to ask you to pray a simple prayer. Remember, of all the things Solomon could have asked to receive from the Lord, he asked for wisdom. Wisdom brought many blessings and insights that few people in this world have ever experienced. God wants to give you His wisdom because He loves you. You are the apple of His eye. As we ask the Lord for His wisdom, let's remember what Christ said in Luke 11:9–13:

> *Ask and it will be given to you; seek and you will find; knock and the door will be opened to you. For everyone who asks receives; he who seeks finds; and to him who knocks, the door will be opened. Which of you fathers, if your son asks for a fish, will give him a snake instead? Or if he asks for an egg, will give him a scorpion? If you then, though you are evil, know how to give good gifts to your children, how much more will your Father in heaven give the Holy Spirit to those who ask him!* (NIV)

We can rest assured that God will give us what we ask for because He is good, and He loves us. Let's pray:

> *Lord, I thank You for bringing me this far in my journey. You have given me purpose and created in me a godly heart. I realize I cannot break the barriers unless You impart Your wisdom to me. Lord, I ask You for wisdom. I ask You for Your perspective in life. Give me the mind of Christ. May Your thoughts be my thoughts. May I see*

*the barriers that confront me with Your eyes. Help me become a person who walks in Your goodness and wisdom. I open my heart to Your new ideas and correction. I open my mind to Your insights and perspective. By faith, I receive Your wisdom.*

*Now, help me to be not only a good and wise person but a strong person as well. Help me to build the strength and endurance necessary to face adversity and overcome the obstacles holding me back from fulfilling the great purpose You have given me. I ask for the power of the Holy Spirit to give me the discipline and strength to break the barriers that stand in the way of what You have destined me to become.*

*Once again, I pledge my life to You and ask You to guide every step I take. I pray all these things in Christ's name. Amen.*

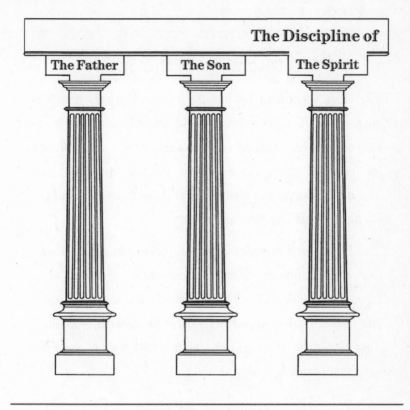

The Discipline of

The Father · The Son · The Spirit

Sufficient Strength

| Godly Discipline | Meditation | The Disciplines of Prayer, Discernment, and Obedience |
| Peace | God Talk | |
| Emotional Resources | Supernatural Strength | |

## The Discipline of the Spirit

*The Holy Spirit breathes life and gives emotional strength to the believer. He gives us peace to overcome the fears that try to keep us from becoming all God has destined us to be. Through the Spirit's leading, our emotional resources increase so we have the strength to overcome our fears and move beyond the barriers. I call this the third pillar.*

*The Holy Spirit provides us with the strength and discipline to put into action everything we know to be good and wise. Doing so will allow us to live a life filled with peace, emotional and spiritual strength, and victory over the adversities we face. Together, these three pillars create a life full of meaning and significance.*

CHAPTER 6

# Peace for Your Soul

*I am certain that my fellow Americans expect that on my induction into the Presidency I will address them with a candor and a decision which the present situation of our Nation impels. This is preeminently the time to speak the truth, the whole truth, frankly and boldly. Nor need we shrink from honestly facing conditions in our country today. This great Nation will endure as it has endured, will revive and will prosper. So, first of all, let me assert my firm belief that the only thing we have to fear is fear itself—nameless, unreasoning, unjustified terror which paralyzes needed efforts to convert retreat into advance. In every dark hour of our national life a leadership of frankness and vigor has met with that understanding and support of the people themselves which is essential to victory. I am convinced that you will again give that support to leadership in these critical days.*

—FRANKLIN D. ROOSEVELT,
*Inaugural Address*
*U.S. Capitol,*
*Washington, D.C.,*
*March 4, 1933*

I T WAS OUR THIRD CRUSADE in the region. We had high expectations because our two previous events in town had been well attended. Several days before the first night of our crusade, our trucks pulled up to the large soccer field and our thirty-member team began to unload the heavy lighting, sound, and electrical gear. Curious children gathered around to see close to twenty tons of equipment being assembled like an Erector Set.

After two days of hard labor, the team completed its task just before we began the first night. At seven o'clock we were under way. As the musical group began the second song, a light drizzle came from the east and began to gently fall on both the stage and everyone in attendance. A gentle drizzle can be refreshing, the shine it puts on everything can be beautiful, but for us, it signaled big trouble. If a light drizzle turns to rain at an outdoor event, you might as well pack up and head home because your crowd has already made its way to the exits.

I started to pray. Minutes before they gave me the microphone, the drizzle turned into small drops. I prayed more fervently. At the end of the drama preceding the message, I walked onto the stage and was greeted with an ovation of raindrops that quickly turned to the proverbial canines and felines.

I believe that God is interactive. By that, I mean He works miracles, brings healing, and does wonders in tangible ways. He's not a distant God. He actively participates in our lives.

Before I began to speak, I prayed, *Oh, Lord, what am I going to do now? Please send the rain in another direction.* I turned my back to the crowd, faced the weather, and continued to pray. Suddenly, the rain stopped as a wind from the west began to blow the rain clouds in the opposite direction. I was in shock—although I didn't let anyone know it. Before I turned and faced the crowd, I said under my breath, "Wow, Lord, this stuff actually works."

Half the crowd stopped in its tracks in amazement, turned, and headed back to the dampened soccer field.

As you can imagine, I began to preach with bold confidence. A new anointing came over me. I felt free to step off the platform and speak among the first few rows of the crowd. I preached one of the best messages ever, and the altar response was amazing.

The next night, the meeting started on time without any threat of rain. Building on the momentum of the previous night, the crusade was developing into a powerful event with about a thousand more in attendance than the first night. About halfway through my message, a man walked onto the lot whom I had never seen before. His head was shaved, and he was wearing a black leather jacket and blue jeans. Since he stood in the back, I didn't notice his demeanor at first.

I had no way of knowing that underneath his leather jacket and tucked into the back of his jeans was a loaded pistol. His finger was on the trigger, and he was stalking me. Within minutes, one of the ushers identified him. He ran over to another usher and told him that Juan, the most wanted drug trafficker in that community, was behind the sound booth. Fear struck the hearts of those who knew his reputation.

He was part of an organized drug ring and was wanted for many crimes as well as for questioning in several homicide cases.

One of the ushers who had circled the perimeter to verify that everything was secure walked up behind Juan and spotted the gun. Soon all the ushers knew Juan was there and that he was armed. At first, none of them wanted to startle any of us who were involved in the event by telling us.

As I came to the close of the message, Juan started to slither his way through the crowd and approached the left side of the stage. He continued with his hand barely out of sight and tucked under his jacket. Considering his reputation, every usher feared he was there to cause havoc—and maybe harm to me. Unaware of his diabolical intentions, I stepped out to the edge of the platform and made the following statement: "Some of you need God's forgiveness. You need His hand to deliver you. You can leave this place free from the bondage in which you live. My only question is, 'Who are you?'"

At that moment, he pulled his hand out from under his jacket—without the gun—and raised it in the air as if to accept my invitation to spiritual freedom. I called those who raised their hands along with Juan to join me at the base of the stage, where I would pray with them. When I came off the platform and met him, a swarm of ushers surrounded us. I had no idea why they responded so aggressively. I had never seen ushers so protective.

He looked at them and said, "What do you want with me? What's your problem? Why don't you guys leave us alone?" Then he turned to me and said, "This has been good for me. It's been a long time since I have talked with the Big Man upstairs." After a very short exchange of words, he turned and left the field.

Driving home that night, my crusade coordinator turned to me and said, "Do you know who that was? It was Juan, a drug dealer, but he came forward tonight because he needed God."

I said, "Praise the Lord."

He continued, "Not only that, but he is wanted by the authorities in this region, and he came forward because he needed to connect with God."

I said, "Praise the Lord."

Then he said, "He is tied to a number of terrible crimes in this area and wanted for questioning in connection with several homicides, but he came forward because he wanted to be set free."

I said, "Praise the Lord."

Finally he said, "Yeah, and tonight he was packing a gun, had his finger on the trigger the entire time, and was going to whack you, but instead he came down to the front because he wanted to change his life."

When he said this, I was speechless. Nothing came out of my mouth. I think he was waiting for one final "Praise the Lord," but none were to be found. I thought, *How in the world could this have happened, and why didn't anyone warn me?*

The next night I watched out for Juan like a rabbit avoiding a predator. Completely distracted by what had happened the previous night, I was preoccupied with whether or not he was going to show up again. To my relief, he didn't. The next night I was on red alert. During the final night, just after the fifth song, he made his entrance. His eyes locked onto me once again as he paced back and forth about twenty yards behind the sound booth.

My heart began to race. Sweat ran down my face. I couldn't see whether he was carrying a weapon or not. It really didn't matter. I simply recognized the same behavior he had displayed three nights before as he paced back and forth like a caged animal. At the close of the message, I gave an invitation for people to turn their lives over to the Lord. Juan came forward. This time, as he began to walk toward the stage, he stared as if he were looking through me. I never saw him blink once. He passed the sound booth and came closer to the stage. Finally, he walked into the altar area. Time stopped. Then he collapsed facedown and began to weep like a baby.

I turned to one of my colleagues and asked him to help me with the situation. Rick was a missionary who had dealt with many unruly people in his twenty years of ministerial experience. He had been an Assemblies of God youth director in Arizona for many years prior to his missionary service. I said, "Rick, would you mind praying this guy through his spiritual difficulties?" Rick kindly agreed. He got down on his hands and knees and began to pray for Juan, who was laid out flat on his face. Juan wept and sobbed for forty-five minutes.

As the service came to a conclusion, Rick finally lifted Juan up, dusted him off, and said, "Now I need to make something absolutely clear to you. You need to start reading the Bible and you need to plug into a local church." Then Rick said, "You can start a new life by helping us break down all this crusade gear." Juan nodded and proceeded to roll up cables, carry speakers, and take pews back to the church. He was the last one to leave the soccer field that night. He'd had a powerful encounter with God.

I stood in admiration of Rick. I never detected any fear in him. I, on the other hand, felt paralyzed. I must have looked like a deer in the headlights of a fast-moving eighteen-wheeler. I knew Juan had come the first night in an attempt to shut down the crusade and hurt me. I confess to you, my friend, fear gripped my heart. Although Juan collapsed and seemed relatively harmless during my invitation at the conclusion of the evening, I had no desire to be within a hundred yards of him. Rick, in contrast, felt secure in his identity and position in Christ. He felt secure with his eternal destination. He felt peace when dealing with one of the most dangerous criminals in the region. He had no concern or fear of being attacked.

I learned a valuable lesson as a result of the incident. The fear I experienced paralyzed me. It drained my emotional resources. Yes, my heart was clean, and I had wisdom. But the fear drained my strength and took away my energy to do what I knew needed to be done. Like most people, when my emotional resources are depleted, I move into survival mode.

I also learned that fear is the most paralyzing force on the face of the planet. It brings us to a standstill. All our potential for breaking barriers and becoming everything we're destined to be is stifled by fear. But the Holy Spirit works against fear. He opposes anxiety. He strengthens our emotional resources so we can become disciplined to break the barriers that hold us back. As the Bible says, "God has not given us a spirit of fear and timidity, but of power, love, and self-discipline" (2 Timothy 1:7 NLT).

The discipline of the Spirit enables us to behave in a controlled and calm way even in difficult or stressful situations. He helps us develop the mental and emotional self-control necessary to change our behavior. In this chapter, we will focus on moving beyond our fears, taking on the mind of Christ, and praying and meditating in order to gain the greatest asset for building strength: God's peace.

Our discipline is not fueled by wisdom or intellect. It is not powered by creativity, driven by a good heart, or controlled by feelings.

The first step in attaining godly strength is to recognize our fears and move away from them by moving toward God's peace. This will give us the strength we need. "The LORD gives strength to his people; the LORD blesses his people with peace" (Psalm 29:11 NIV).

## NO FEAR!

Let's consider the *Star Wars* movie plots. Whenever the Rebel Alliance engaged the Galactic Empire warships in battle, in critical times they had to redirect all power to the shields protecting the ship. However, doing so left other vital sections of the starship, such as life support, air filtration, and propulsion, exposed and vulnerable. Fear does the same to us. Whenever we redirect all of our energies to our defense system, our energy levels are drained and can leave other emotional areas of our lives defenseless. As a result, we spend countless hours in fear, anxiety, and preoccupation, and we feel exhausted.

Fear is one of the most powerful motivating factors we have today. It can make us diet. It can make us run or hide. It can make us pay our bills. It might prevent us from flying, driving, or going out at night. It can motivate a lying person to tell the truth. It modifies behavior. But with time, fear wears off. Its effect on us eventually diminishes. For instance, many who have had open-heart surgery change their diet, begin to exercise, and reduce their stress. But eventually, some fall back into old eating habits, stop exercising, and take on more work than ever. Why? Their fear of death has subsided and no longer motivates them to be disciplined.

Fear of death cannot be our primary motivating force. Anxiety cannot be our primary motivating force. Adrenaline cannot be our primary motivating force. A drive for success cannot be our primary motivating force.

We need to push aside anxiety and fear as our primary motivators and become pursuers of God's peace. All our emotional security about who we are, what our future holds, and where we will spend eternity must be based upon God's peace for our lives. "The peace of God, which transcends all understanding, will guard your hearts and your minds in Christ Jesus" (Philippians 4:7 NIV).

So how do we attain the peace of God? First, keep in mind what we discussed in the introduction. We must stay focused on God's purpose for our lives. Fulfilling the destiny God has laid out for us brings eternal peace. It helps bring overall serenity during times of anxiety and confusion. The apostle Paul says in Philippians 3:14, "I press on toward the goal to win the prize for which God has called me heavenward in Christ Jesus" (NIV). Paul was one of the most influential leaders of the first-century church. He wrote a good portion of the New Testament. Paul kept the purpose of God for his life clear. He never lost sight of it.

Paul faced countless struggles and persecution. He was thrown into prison. He was shipwrecked and bitten by a poisonous snake. He ended up sentenced to death for his faith in Christ. No matter what came his way, he remembered God's purpose and divine will for his life. Paul never suffered a nervous breakdown, never cursed God, and never complained that life wasn't fair. Instead, he stayed true to the message he preached. He lived every minute in accordance with the purpose God gave him. That's why the first pillar is so important. It acts as our anchor and reminds us who we are in Christ.

Like Paul, if we understand God's purpose for our lives and live toward His goal for us, we are well on our way to attaining His peace. Once we have a clear understanding of our God-given purpose, the next step in attaining peace is to have the mind of Christ. We do this by working diligently with God to change our self-talk.

## GOD-TALK

For the purposes of this section, I would like to use the term God-talk to describe what I call godly self-talk, that is, having God's thoughts in our minds.

After we discover God's purpose for our lives, we must begin to rewrite the scripts in our minds that fill us with fear. They must be replaced with healthy self-talk taken from God's Word. Negative self-talk produces feelings of instability and worry, but it can be managed and rewritten so that in times of turbulence we can walk in peace and serenity. As God's thoughts become ours, we begin to walk in confidence and tranquillity. We do this by learning, accepting, and applying what God thinks about us as revealed in His Word.

As you renew your mind by reading God's Word, His peace begins to fill your heart. The result will be a life filled with joy and meaningful connection between you and God. Ultimately, you will see your life dramatically change, and you will gain the necessary stability to live a disciplined life.

In order to rewrite the scripts in our minds, we need to have a practical approach. One of the healthiest ways to respond to our feelings of anxiety and fear is to read again what God says about us in the Bible. I have an exercise that has helped me throughout the years. I take a piece of paper and draw a line down the middle. On the left side I write down the negative self-talk I hear in my head during times of turmoil or stress. I don't leave anything out. It doesn't matter how ridiculous it sounds. Every thought contrary to what God thinks about me is written down. I do not stop until I have emptied my soul out on paper. Once I have written down everything that seems to have a destructive pattern in my thoughts, I lay my pen down and ask God to help me see things from His perspective. I ask Him to help me see myself as He sees me.

On the right side of the paper, I write down what God says about me in His Word. I describe my attributes and qualities according to Him. After all, the Bible says in Romans 9:26 that we are created in God's image and that we were destined to become the sons and daughters of God. Who knows his offspring better than a father? With that in mind, I write down what God says are my qualities as His son.

The Bible says God loves me and cares deeply about me. He cares about my well-being. He makes provision for me and desires for me to reach my greatest potential. He has created me with a purpose and wants me to complete it. I cannot do anything to impress Him or make Him love me more. His love is solid. It is consistent. It is not dependent upon my actions. The Bible says Jesus came to earth and died for all my transgressions. He died in my place. He sees me as a worthy person, someone who has eternal worth. If God loves me just the way I am with blemishes and all, who I am to suggest that I am unlovable? Who am I to question His authority to proclaim who and what I am?

You, my friend, are no different. This is exactly how God feels about you. He loves you. You cannot do anything to make God love you more. It is impossible for you to impress Him. It matters not what you have done. It matters not how good or bad you are. God sees you with great potential for becoming His son or daughter. You have incredible worth and eternal value.

For this reason He sent His Son to die on a cross for you—because He sees you as worthy of redemption. If God would send His Son to help you two thousand years ago, why would He leave the job half finished and not help you today? God is faithful to complete what He has started. First Thessalonians 5:24 says, "The one who calls you is faithful and he will do it" (NIV). You, my friend, are no exception to that rule.

Read the following Scriptures regarding what God thinks of His people. As a son or daughter of God, these verses are meant to edify and encourage you:

- In a desert land he found him, in a barren and
  howling waste. He shielded him and cared for him;

he guarded him as the apple of his eye. (Deuteronomy 32:10 NIV)

- This is what the LORD Almighty says: "Whoever touches you touches the apple of his eye." (Zechariah 2:8 NIV)
- Keep me as the apple of your eye; hide me in the shadow of your wings. (Psalm 17:8 NIV)
- The Father himself loves you because you have loved me and have believed that I came from God. (John 16:27 NIV)
- I have been crucified with Christ and I no longer live, but Christ lives in me. The life I live in the body, I live by faith in the Son of God, who loved me and gave himself for me. (Galatians 2:20 NIV)
- Know therefore that the LORD your God is God; he is the faithful God, keeping his covenant of love to a thousand generations of those who love him and keep his commands. (Deuteronomy 7:9 NIV)
- This is how God showed his love among us: He sent his one and only Son into the world that we might live through him. This is love: not that we loved God, but that he loved us and sent his Son as an atoning sacrifice for our sins. Dear friends, since God so loved us, we also ought to love one another. (1 John 4:9–11 NIV)

## EXERCISE YOUR GOD-TALK

Begin to build your self-esteem by using God-talk. Make His thoughts your thoughts. He inspired these Bible verses to encourage and help you, so take advantage of them. Make God your partner and rewrite your self-talk. Rewrite the way you think. Reformat the hard drive in your head. Reinvent your internal dialogue.

The apostle Paul recognized our great need to change our preconceptions. He writes in Romans 12:2, "Do not conform any longer to the pattern of this world, but be transformed by the renewing of your mind. Then you will be able to test and approve what God's will is—his good, pleasing and perfect will" (NIV).

As I mentioned above, begin by writing out your self-talk. Then contrast it with what God says about you in His Word. Tell yourself periodically throughout the day how God thinks and feels about you. After several days, you will notice a significant difference in your attitudes, feelings, and emotional resources. Again, what you are trying to do is rerecord the script in your mind to replace the negative self-talk that drains your emotional resources.

If you feel somewhat adventurous, perhaps you might take the method a step further. Write out what the Bible says about you as a script. Then record it onto your iPod or any MP3 player. Each morning as you begin your day, listen to what God says about you from a source you can trust.

You do not have to continue your patterns of fear, anxiety, and stress. Your future is not etched in stone. God can change the course of your destiny. When your mind says you are not worthy or you are stupid or fat or less of a person, recite what God says about you. Replace the lies Satan would have you believe with the truth of what God says about you. Read God's Word. Listen to what He says about those who love and follow

Him. As you begin to listen to God-talk and absorb it into your mind, you will notice a great transformation taking place within you. Peace will begin to permeate your mind and spirit. You will notice your spiritual resources beginning to gain strength, and as a result, your emotional resources will become recharged. The discipline you need to break the barriers comes as the Spirit of God continues to work in you and edify you.

## PICTURE THIS

Prayer and meditation on God's Word are vital for attaining God's peace. Regardless of the challenges that confront you, I have good news for you. No matter what is happening in your life, you can always go to the Lord in prayer. Of all the things you can do, this is the most essential. When you're in search of peace and can't sleep at night, talk to God. When your mind is racing and you can't calm the anxious voices in your head, ask God for help. When you can't stop thinking about your financial problems and your fears only intensify, open up the communication lines with heaven and say, "Lord, You are the Prince of Peace. Fill me with Your peace."

You will sense His presence. You will sense His peace.

Perhaps you don't have the energy to lift up your voice and ask God for help. Maybe you don't know what to pray. You might not have the emotional energy to try. If that's how you feel, turn to the Spirit and ask Him for help. When we don't know what to pray, when we feel paralyzed and anxious, when our emotional gas tank is on empty, the Holy Spirit intercedes for us. He comes to our assistance when we're broken down along the road of life. Paul sums it up well: "The Spirit helps us in our weakness. We do not know what we ought to pray for, but the Spirit himself intercedes for us with groans that words cannot express" (Romans 8:26 NIV).

Like prayer, meditation brings comfort and stability. For centuries, people have meditated on different parts of the Bible. The Psalms, Proverbs, and stories from both the Old and the New Testaments are wonderful for meditation. After I read a passage of Scripture, I go over the biblical story I read and imagine myself as one of the characters. Like a movie, I imagine the culture, the setting, and the individual personalities.

One of my favorite stories to meditate on is found in the New Testament. On the side of the road is a man who was born blind. His name is Bartimaeus. The town is small, and everyone knows him. He has been sitting on the roadside each day for many years, asking for money. Over time, the sun has darkened his skin, and because of his condition he is unable to adequately care for his appearance.

The day begins like any other. The smells of nearby farm animals fill the town as slow-moving foot traffic kicks up dust along the dirt road. With a few scattered clouds the temperature is about eighty-three degrees. The noon hour is fast approaching, and the town women begin preparing for lunch. Few people pay attention to the blind beggar.

Then an unusual noise begins to rise in Bartimaeus's direction. As each minute passes, his curiosity grows. At first, he is unable to distinguish the distant clatter. After several minutes, he can tell it is no small group of people headed his way. Instead, hundreds of people are moving like a slow herd through the center of town. People begin to line up along the side of the road in hopes of discovering who is at the center of the crowd. Scattered conversations along the road ask, "Is it a politician or a religious leader? Who could it be?" The excitement builds, but Bartimaeus cannot see anything. He can rely only on his hearing.

In hopes of learning more about what is driving the large crowd in a small town, he moves his walking stick, tapping the ground around his mat in an attempt to discover a foot or leg. Someone next to him blurts, "Ouch!"

"Pardon me," Bartimaeus replies. "Can you tell me what is causing all the noise I hear coming our way?"

"The people up the road seem to think it is the famous healer. The One they think might be the Messiah. They call him 'Jesus of Nazareth,'" replies his neighbor. "Yes, yes, as a matter of fact it is He. Jesus of Nazareth is passing by."

Surprised and enthused, Bartimaeus asks himself, *What? Jesus of Nazareth? The great healer? The Messiah sent from God to help Israel? He's here in my town, and walking down my street?* The blind man is enthralled. The only person who heals blind people is Jesus. *Perhaps He will heal me,* Bartimaeus thinks optimistically.

As the crowd approaches, the lonely beggar begins to shout with the rest of those lined up along the road, "Jesus! Jesus! Jesus!" As Christ comes within fifty feet, Bartimaeus calls out at the top of his lungs, "Jesus, Son of David, have mercy on me!"

The people around him try to quiet him. "He is the Messiah. He has no interest in you. You are not important!"

But he raises his voice with greater desperation. "Jesus, Son of David, have mercy on me!"

All of a sudden, Jesus stops and turns around. Time stands still. Everything around Bartimaeus and Jesus freezes. The two of them are connected. Somehow, some way, Jesus hears the man's plea. He manages to filter out all the other conversations, cheers, and ambient noise. He focuses on a simple man's request.

He turns to His disciples and says with authority, "Bring him to Me." Without hesitation, two of the disciples are dispatched like a special forces team on a mission. With ease, they penetrate the pressing crowd.

When those who tried to quiet Bartimaeus see the disciples coming their way, they instantly become his best friends. "Hey, cheer up. The Master is calling you. This is your lucky day. Up onto your feet." Then they help him stand and kindly hand him over to the disciples, who guide him to Christ. A path is opened for the blind man to meet Jesus. The crowd's chatter turns to silence. Just Jesus and Bartimaeus stand in a circle with hundreds of people quietly looking onward. Jesus looks sternly at the beggar and pauses for a few brief seconds.

Although Bartimaeus cannot see, he feels as though Christ is looking into his soul. Warmth washes over him as his optic nerves are touched by an orange glow like looking at the sun with your eyes closed. Standing at the center of town, standing in the center of a large crowd, standing as the center of attention, his heart is racing. Then Jesus asks the question Bartimaeus has been waiting to hear his entire life: "What do you want Me to do for you?"

Without hesitation he says, "I want to regain my sight."

Jesus stretches out His hand and says, "Receive your sight; your faith has healed you." Touching the blind man's face sparks an immediate molecular reaction. The optic nerves become stimulated and begin to send signals back to the brain for the first time. Colors, dimensions, and perspectives are suddenly interpreted by the cerebral cortex. A whole new world appears before the man's newly developed eyes. Jesus smiles, winks, and says, "Take care of yourself, and remember to give God the glory!"

The story of Bartimaeus that appears in Mark 10:46–52 is much shorter than what I just described. It runs seven verses in

Breaking the Barriers

all. So why do I stretch out the story? It helps me meditate on Scripture. It helps me connect with God. As the exercise develops, I try to smell the odors, see even more of the scenery, and visualize even more of the people. I try to envision myself there as it happened. It helps me understand Christ's love and concern for people. I imagine myself as Bartimaeus or one of the disciples who brought the blind man to Christ, or one of the other major characters in the story.

As I play the part of Bartimaeus, I imagine the Lord healing my body, helping me overcome any anxiety or fear, giving me insight to break my financial barriers, or helping me to be a better husband and father. When I can visualize Christ helping me and showing His support, peace begins to fill my heart. My emotional reservoir begins to fill up.

Afterward, I remind myself that if Christ was willing to stop and help out a lonely beggar, for example, He would surely be willing to help me. Romans 8:31 says, "If God is for us, who can be against us?" (NIV). If God is on my side, it doesn't matter who or what is against me. If Christ is for me, then I can rest in His peace.

The peace of God is the most stabilizing force on the face of the planet. It's the antithesis of anxiety. It's being free from mental, spiritual, and emotional turbulence. God's peace is our starting point for building up our emotional resources, which gives us the strength to break barriers.

## FASTEN YOUR SEAT BELTS AND HOLD ON FOR DEAR LIFE

Ever since I was a teenager, I was afraid of flying. I had never canceled a flight on account of my fears; however, every time I walked down the Jetway, I began to pray. As I crossed the threshold to enter the aircraft, I would place my hand on the outside of the fuselage and ask the Lord to protect the plane from any mechanical failures and pilot errors. During each flight, I was a nervous wreck.

One night I was on a flight from Los Angeles to San José, Costa Rica. We had a short layover in Guatemala City. After an hour of refueling and unloading and loading of passengers, we continued on our way. At approximately 6:00 a.m., the plane began to taxi down the long stretch of concrete until we made a 180-degree turn and lined up for takeoff. The pilot received the green light from the control tower to make our departure. The Boeing 757 motors began to rev up. The pilot released the brakes, and we began to head down the runway. It seemed as though the thrust of the motors sucked everyone into their seats a bit more than normal. With each second, the g-forces increased until we were finally airborne.

For the first several thousand feet, we were flying through overcast skies. At about 7,000 feet, the nose of the 240,000-pound metallic bird poked through the clouds, and we could see the sun for the first time that day. What a beautiful sight it was! There is nothing like emerging through the clouds and seeing crystal blue skies. We were taking off to the north, so we started to bank to the right, heading south to San José.

The flight attendants pulled out their carts and began serving coffee and those famous airline peanuts that have all but disappeared. All of a sudden, the pilot made an announcement, the one that we all love to hear: "All flight attendants, please be seated immediately with your seat belts fastened." In my mind that means only one thing: we are about to fly through the most unstable air in the world. Even though flight attendants are experts at negotiating their way down the aisle through turbulence, the storm we were about to fly into was out of their league. So they quickly returned their carts to the galley and fastened their seat belts.

All at once, the plane dropped what seemed to be thirty feet and began to dance all over the sky. In all my years of flying, I have never experienced such a ride. Pilots tell me there are three stages of turbulence: light, moderate, and *hold on for dear life*. We were definitely experiencing stage three!

The aircraft began to tilt to the right and descended quickly. People in the main cabin screamed. The lady sitting next to me saw her coffee cup float into the air and spill all over her lap. In the midst of the chaos, for some strange reason, the lady on the other side of the aisle thought it was the appropriate time to pull out her makeup bag and put on some lipstick. When I saw the creative "Sassy Spice"–colored red design covering parts of her nose and cheeks, it brought a split-second smile to my face. There was a bit of good news through it all, though: no one was standing in line to use the restroom.

All of this, at 500 miles per hour!

The turbulence continued and so did the voices of panic in my head. I'm not sure what's worse—death or the fear of death. Finally, out of desperation, I closed my eyes, squeezed the armrests, and began to pray. My prayer didn't sound like that of a powerful man of faith. It definitely didn't sound authoritative. Instead, it probably sounded something like, "Help me, God. I really don't want to crash into the Central American jungle!"

Then a Scripture verse came to mind. "Do not fear, for I am with you; do not be dismayed, for I am your God. I will strengthen you and help you; I will uphold you with my righteous right hand" (Isaiah 41:10 NIV). At that moment God helped me turn a corner, a corner in my faith and in my strength. His presence came to me while I prayed, while I thought about that verse. The thoughts of Christ began to flow through my mind as the Spirit brought me comfort and stability. I felt a strong impression in my heart, as if He was saying, "All right, all right, just calm down. Nothing is going to happen to this aircraft. I will uphold you with My righteous right hand."

The third pillar, the discipline of the Spirit, gives us the strength to behave in a controlled and calm way even in a difficult or stressful situation. The Spirit helped me experience His peace in spite of the fact that I was in exactly that—a difficult, stressful situation.

As I continued to pray, something wonderful happened. The plane began to level off. It felt as if we had landed. There was absolutely no movement whatsoever, and within minutes, the flight attendants resumed their in-flight service. They kindly helped my neighbor clean the spilled coffee, and they brought a wet towel to help the newly discovered makeup artist as well. The flight remained pleasant until we reached our destination.

I learned several important lessons from this experience. My life is ultimately in God's hands. If I have completed my purpose here on earth, then there is no need to be here any longer. If I haven't, then God will keep me around until I have. There, at thirty-five thousand feet, I was reconnected to God's purpose for my life.

Also, God helped me to see that His self-talk is better for me than my own. Instead of entertaining thoughts of panic, I decided to listen to what God had to say about the situation.

Finally, He showed me that when everything flies out of control, sometimes all we can do is pray. Sometimes we can't call 911. Sometimes there is no immediate solution. All we can do is call on His name, and He hears us. This is great news. In the midst of the storm, when we have nothing left, He is more than willing to embrace us and give us peace.

Something else miraculous happened on that flight. The Spirit helped me experience peace in the midst of the storm, and as a result, my empty emotional reservoir filled up again. My strength returned, and with it, my ability to see clearly. Today, I am no longer a slave to the fear of flying.

Why was that such an important breakthrough? It would be very difficult to move forward in my life without traveling. How could I travel internationally without getting on a plane? The Spirit gave me peace that overcame the barrier!

Many of the pages of this book were written at thirty-five thousand feet. Although at times I flew through turbulent weather, I experienced God's peace and found the discipline to bring this book to you.

Paul understood how important peace is for those who face barriers. In Romans 8:6, he wrote: "The mind of sinful man is death, but the mind controlled by the Spirit is life and peace" (NIV). He continues in verse 15: "You did not receive a spirit that makes you a slave again to fear, but you received the Spirit of sonship. And by him we cry, 'Abba, Father'" (NIV).

Have you ever felt so drained by the pressures of life that you had nothing left to give? Have you ever felt as if your strength has dwindled to nothing? If so, the best way to strengthen your emotional resources is to ask God for His peace. As you experience His peace, you'll have the energy to put into action what you know to be good and wise.

Partnering with God in the turbulence of life brings serenity, stability, and peace for our souls.

## BE RIGHT, KNOW RIGHT, DO RIGHT

Having discipline is doing what you know is right in the midst of an emotional storm. It is doing what you know is right in the midst of apathy. It means doing what you know is right when no one is willing to support you. Through valleys and over mountains, through highs and lows and in the face of fear and panic, the discipline of the Spirit gives us the strength to consistently implement what we know is good and wise.

You were created with great purpose and destiny. God loves you and has wonderful plans for your life. He made you with talents and gifts. No one else was made like you. You, my friend, are unique, created by God to reach your greatest potential and give glory to God.

As this chapter comes to a close, I want to encourage you to take care of yourself as God would. Take care of your spirit by reading the Bible, praying, and worshiping the Lord. Take care of your emotions by finding God's peace and replacing the negative self-talk in your head with God's thoughts. Finally, I would like to add something equally important, although I recognize it belongs in another book. I encourage you to take care of your body by eating right, exercising appropriately, and getting enough rest and sleep. Practicing all these habits will help to establish the discipline of God in your life.

The next chapter focuses on ways to unleash the power of the Spirit in our lives. We'll look at helpful insights for developing spiritual self-discipline in all areas of life. When we conclude, the third pillar will be set. The three pillars working together in your life give you the power to be right, know right, and do right. Together, they enable you to break every barrier. And as a result of living the principles set forth in this book, you will experience a life filled with meaning and significance!

Let us turn our hearts toward the Lord and ask for help to be disciplined people who have the strength to implement what is good and wise. As you pray this prayer, imagine the Lord smiling in acceptance of your petition.

*Dear Lord, once again I ask You for help. So many times I find myself weak and unable to implement what I know is right. Help me to move away from my fears and anxieties so You can build my emotional strength. I want my self-esteem to be built upon Your confidence and the way You feel about me. Many times, I feel unworthy as a person and that others are better than I am. I know Your Word says You love me all the same. So change the way I think and feel. I know I cannot do this alone. I need Your help. Help me to have Your thoughts. Help me to see myself as a child of God. The recording in my head has been contaminated with destructive patterns that tear me down. My self-talk has been negative, and I know You desire to change the way I think. You, O Lord, can help me change.*

*I ask You to build my confidence and help me to become a disciplined person who is godly. I want to be someone who is good and wise, as You intended me to be. Above all, help me to exalt Your name in every area of my life, and may every barrier I break bring glory and honor to Your name. I ask these things in Christ's name. Amen.*

CHAPTER 7

# Unleashing the Power of the Spirit in Your Life

THE ACCIDENT WAS HORRIFIC. On Sunday at approximately 11:00 a.m., a dump truck crossed over the double yellow line and converted the 2000 Land Rover Defender into a pile of rubble. Our dear friend and the official photographer of our crusades, Armando Rojas, was pinned inside for more than twenty minutes as firefighters tried to extract him from the crushed vehicle. The dump truck was carrying dirt and heading to a remote location to unload it. As the driver came around a bend in the highway, the weight of his load caused the front axle to snap in two. The two front tires immediately broke off, forcing the thirty-ton truck to swerve out of control and into oncoming traffic.

The collision was head-on, and it was a miracle Armando wasn't instantly killed. He was in a difficult position, unconscious and in need of immediate medical attention, but still breathing. Once he was freed, the paramedics rushed him to a state hospital, where they discovered that one of his lungs was punctured and that there were several other severe fractures throughout his body.

I received the news as I landed in Los Angeles to catch my connection to Costa Rica.

My heart was gripped by the message: Armando's condition was worsening. At first, the doctors thought they would have to amputate one of his arms. They later discovered it was a moot point: Armando's kidneys were shutting down—the physicians believed he would die.

After flying for nearly ten hours, I finally arrived in Costa Rica at 7:15 Monday morning. I had five messages from various sources asking if I could go to the hospital and pray for Armando. His two brothers and sister were in shock. His entire staff was in disbelief. Regrettably, I was fighting a head cold and was not permitted to enter the hospital. Little did I know it would be my only opportunity to see him. The next morning, his condition continued to decline. I called Alex, his brother, and told him I was too ill to enter the hospital. He kindly pardoned me.

Wednesday morning at approximately eight o'clock, Armando passed into eternity. The members of our crusade team couldn't believe it. It sent shock waves through the entire country. Armando's death was difficult to fathom—the man who had snapped every altar call picture, who had traveled to every crusade city, including those in other countries, and who had made so many of us smile with his kindness and warmth, was no longer with us. He had gone on to be with the Lord.

Sitting at the funeral, I was immediately taken back to the first time I had met Armando. It was at his photography studio in the fall of 1996. He was one of the finest photographers in Latin America. We had asked him to shoot our family photo. I later solicited his services to come to our next crusade and take pictures.

The first crusade he photographed was in Barranca, Costa Rica. Thousands of people had come to hear the good news of

Christ. He photographed hundreds upon hundreds of people making first-time decisions dedicating their lives to the Lord. Afterward he said, "I have never been in any kind of event like this. I haven't been inside a church since I was a kid. I got some good 'vibes' from being here tonight." Of course I knew what that meant. God was beginning to knock on the door of his heart.

I decided Armando should be our official photographer. I gave him a ministerial T-shirt and hat. Although he had not made a commitment to Christ, I knew God had something wonderful in store for his life. As the years passed, from time to time he would share with me the struggles he was dealing with. He called me once and asked me to come into his office and pray for him so he could stop drinking. Slowly but surely, Armando was beginning to recognize he needed Jesus to break his chains and deliver him.

Finally one night we were in one of our largest crusades ever. It was at an indoor arena located several miles from the heart of a major metropolitan city. The last night of the crusade, I gave an altar call and watched several thousand people come forward for salvation. I thought to myself, *This is great! Surely Armando will capture this on film better than anyone else!*

As I looked out toward the sound booth, I saw Armando's camera lying next to the mixer. I was puzzled. I motioned to our sound engineer: *Where is Armando?* He pointed back at me. I looked down front. There he was, standing five feet in front of me, with tears streaming down his face, gloriously accepting Christ and asking God for forgiveness. I came down off the platform and prayed with him. What a moving experience!

With each passing crusade, I saw Armando's faith deepening, I saw his character changing, I saw his faith increasing, I saw him growing in Christ. Each time I went to his studio to pick up a batch of crusade photos, he met me with hugs and great enthusiasm.

I watched the chains of alcoholism break by the power of God. I watched the bondage of addictive behavior begin to shatter. I watched God put his life back together and carry him to even greater heights as one of the world's most talented photographers. Of all his accomplishments, however, the greatest was attaining a relationship with Christ.

As I sat in the funeral service, I thought about the last time I had spoken to him. It was much like the first time I had met him in his studio. Two months to the day prior to his accident, my wife, our girls, and I went in for another family session. He accepted us with great hospitality as usual. But before we left, he turned to me and said, "Jason, let's have a word of prayer together." What a great contrast from the first time I had met him. What a godly transformation. Only God can change lives like that.

After the night he made a commitment to Christ, Armando had begun to pray, read God's Word, and believe for victory over the barrier of alcoholism. As a result, the heart of God started to form inside him. He listened to the godly advice of others and thus took on godly wisdom.

When I first met him, he was full of anxiety and had difficulty managing his emotions. Through his connection with Christ, he found the peace of God, which raised the level of his emotional resources. As he developed spiritual self-discipline, his endurance began to build. He became more productive and creative. Soon, he was consistently implementing what he knew was godly and wise. As God began to help him become disciplined, he was able to move beyond the barrier of alcoholism and focus on the divine purpose God laid out for him.

As a devout follower of Christ, he traveled to various countries of Latin America as well as the United States, winning awards and capturing with his thirty-five-millimeter camera what few human eyes have seen. By age forty-seven, Armando Rojas was arguably the finest photographer in Central America.

In spite of all his success and international notoriety, he never allowed his studio to service exclusively the wealthy and affluent. Instead, he continued to photograph every school that asked him to take individual student and class pictures. He took every school picture of my girls until the day he died. Without a doubt, Armando Rojas broke his barriers, overcame adversity, and reached his greatest potential. In his final years, he became highly conscious that God had given him his ability to beautifully capture everyday life with a Nikon.

Armando's story shows us that in addition to a godly heart and wisdom, to break the barriers we also need God's discipline to execute what we know is good and wise.

Having godly discipline is the ability to consistently implement what we know to be God's purpose for our lives. Once we have a godly heart and godly wisdom, we can begin to build the strength and discipline of the Holy Spirit to complete whatever task we face.

## PRACTICAL INSIGHTS FOR DEVELOPING SPIRITUAL SELF-DISCIPLINE

Whenever the term "spiritual self-discipline" comes to mind, most of us imagine the classics such as prayer, Bible study, Scripture memorization, fellowship, fasting, and sharing our faith. Although we've covered several of these subjects in some form or another in previous chapters, they are worth revisiting. At this point in our journey, I must ask the question: *What do you need to know in order to break barriers?* The following disciplines promise to be very helpful in your quest to firmly establish the third pillar, and my hope is that you will apply them to all areas of life. These disciplines will empower you to gain victory over the challenges you face. Let's start with the most essential, prayer.

## 1. The Discipline of Prayer

Of all the spiritual disciplines, prayer is the most fundamental and necessary. It is the primary way we communicate with God. Prayer is how we express our worship, thanksgiving, confession, intercession, and desires to our heavenly Father.

Why is prayer so important? It is absolutely crucial in developing our connection with God. Without prayer, we can't maintain our relationship with Him. There is no substitute. And besides, He wants us to pray (see 1 Thessalonians 5:16–18).

Prayer brings guidance and direction and ushers us into God's presence regardless of where we are. Think about that for a moment. No matter what issue you face, you can always pray about it. You can ask the Lord for His guidance and direction. And you can expect an answer. Scripture says, "Be assured that from the first day we heard of you, we haven't stopped praying for you, asking God to give you wise minds and spirits attuned to his will, and so acquire a thorough understanding of the ways in which God works" (Colossians 1:9 *The Message*).

Prayer can change circumstances. It can change people. And it definitely changes us. Prayer aligns our will with God's so that we can see what is good and wise.

Jesus made prayer a priority in His life. For Him, prayer wasn't just an occasional encounter with God. It was His custom. He made a daily commitment to spend time with His heavenly Father: "Jesus often withdrew to lonely places and prayed" (Luke 5:16 NIV).

Sometimes He prayed in the morning (see Mark 1:35). Sometimes He prayed at night (see Matthew 14:23). Jesus prayed before and after big events, in the middle of the desert, in the garden, and while He was in lonely places. His example has taught me an important lesson: no time is the wrong time to pray, and no time is better than now! He serves as a wonderful role model for living a disciplined life of prayer.

## WHEN THERE SEEMS TO BE NO WAY OUT

"There's absolutely no way you're getting back to the United States this week." Those were the words of a spokesperson working for a U.S. carrier at the International Airport in Buenos Aires. The thirty-year-old Argentine woman felt very confident that the airline wasn't going to fly for at least eight days. "You can leave from this country on another carrier, but no flights are heading to the United States." My wife and I stood at the ticket counter with bags in hand and feeling disappointed. Considering the horrific acts that had occurred prior to our return flight, it was understandable. The day before, nineteen hijackers had commandeered four airplanes in the most awful terrorist attacks in history, and as a result of the international crisis, all flights to the United States were canceled or diverted. After spending a memorable week in Argentina, we were stuck, and no matter what we did, there seemed to be no way out.

Before arriving in Argentina, we left Costa Rica, flew through Los Angeles, and left our three little girls with grandparents before the eleven-hour flight over the curve of the earth. The evangelistic outreach and ministerial conference were refreshing, but our time came to an abrupt and disturbing end. Most who watched the shocking slow-motion replays of planes flying into buildings wanted to be close to family. Cindee and I were no exception. All we could think about was going home and holding our daughters.

We needed God's help. We needed His direction. So I prayed, my wife prayed, and we decided to call for spiritual reinforcement.

We needed God to open a door. Reaching out to Him through prayer was the only way that door would open. Cindee sat down at a three-dollar-per-minute Internet-access computer and hammered out an e-mail to her father. It explained our predicament and asked him to share it with anyone who would take our need before the Lord. He immediately forwarded it to a special group of intercessors who had a disciplined prayer life. With one click of the mouse, hundreds of people around the world began to pray for our situation.

Soon night came, and more people joined the prayer chain.

Then the Lord gave me an idea. "Perhaps we shouldn't look for a flight to Los Angeles. Maybe the best thing would be to fly to Tijuana and walk across the border."

At 9:00 p.m., I received a call from a local travel agent saying there was a flight heading from Argentina to Mexico City at 1:30 in the morning. I said, "We'll take it!" The red-eye took us back to the North American continent. I must admit, flying on September 13, 2001, was a bit nerve-racking. For nine solid hours, I never took my eyes off the cockpit door.

Around the world, people continued to pray for us. Some had the discipline to pray in the early hours of the morning, just like the Lord. They asked God to keep us safe during our flight and to help us find a flight from Mexico City to Tijuana the next day. Even though there were no available seats for the last leg, they prayed for an open door.

After we landed in Mexico City, I called my father-in-law and asked him to e-mail the intercessors an update. They continued to pray. We called our travel agent, expecting to hear that there were no seats available. Instead, she said, "You might be able to fly standby, but there's only one problem. The last flight leaving for Tijuana is on the other side of the Mexico City airport, and it's boarding now!" Before she finished her sentence I hung up, and we ran as fast as we could in spite of our present altitude of almost eight thousand feet above sea level. We approached the gate out of breath just before they closed the door. Indeed, there were two seats available, one in the front of the aircraft, the other in the back. The flight of three hours and fifteen minutes took us to the city nestled in the upper western corner of Mexico. It was a stone's throw to the San Diego border.

My father-in-law drove to Tijuana and picked us up. We headed to the border, where scores of FBI agents carefully examined each person and vehicle. After waiting in line for two long hours, we finally crossed the border. That night we joined our girls, and within a week we were back in Costa Rica. When people ask me how we made it back, I respond: "We rode home on the backs of the prayers of those who live a disciplined spiritual life." Prayer works. It changes circumstances. It changes people. It definitely changes us.

Make prayer a daily discipline, and every area of your life will greatly benefit. If you desire to break the barriers that separate you from becoming all God has destined you to be, ask the Lord for guidance and direction every day. "The LORD is far from the wicked but he hears the prayer of the righteous" (Proverbs 15:29 NIV).

This is the basis upon which we build all the other spiritual self-disciplines. Building a disciplined prayer life opens the lines of communication with God so you can develop the next discipline: hearing God's voice. It's one thing to talk to God. It's another thing to hear Him.

## 2. The Discipline of Hearing God's Voice

*How do you know when God speaks to you?* This is the one question people ask me more than any other. No matter how we slice it, the answer is different for everyone, because God speaks to each of us in different ways.

Let me begin by saying it is God's will that you fine-tune your spiritual ears to hear His direction for your life. The Bible says, "Listen for GOD's voice in everything you do, everywhere you go; he's the one who will keep you on track" (Proverbs 3:6 *The Message*). The ability to discern His voice will help you break barriers and overcome adversity, and I believe God warmly desires to help you develop this wonderful discipline.

In the Bible, the phrase "The Lord said" or "God said" appears more than 350 times. We can be assured that God continues to communicate with us today, for He says, "My sheep listen to my voice" (John 10:27 NIV). The question still remains, though: How do we know when it's the Lord who is speaking to us?

There are four biblical ways to help you discern if the Lord is speaking to you. These biblical standards serve as filters, and we need godly wisdom to use them correctly. That's why having the second pillar firmly established in our lives is vital. Godly wisdom helps us separate God's voice from the nonsense we conjure up or get from someone else. I will discuss these filters in a few moments.

Now, we might sense that the Lord is speaking to us through Scripture. This is perhaps the most common way. We read something that jumps off the pages and think, *Wow, that's just what I needed to hear.* Perhaps we listen to a sermon and say to ourselves, *He was talking directly to me. That message changed my life!* Other times we might be alone and feel a strong impression that God wants us to do something or embrace a specific truth. For the purposes of this section about developing spiritual self-discipline, I will talk about what is commonly referred to as "that still, small voice."

In my case, I have never heard a thunderous audible voice saying, "Thus saith the Lord!" That would be great, but such a privilege has never come my way. Rather, God speaks to me in the form of a still, small voice—an impression—that cannot be dismissed. I can't explain it away, and with time it grows.

We might describe it as a thought, conviction, or direction that connects with what is commonly called our sixth sense and aligns with what we believe is right. It flows in harmony with the first pillar, our mission and reason for being. Let me identify and explain the filters.

*Filter One:* When I get an impression, I ask myself a series of questions to confirm whether what I sense is from God or simply the pizza I had the night before. First, I compare the impression to my perception of God. Is this something my heavenly Father would say to me? Is it characteristic of Him? Does it line up with my golden thread? Is it congruent with the first, second, and third pillars in my life? Is this something I should look up in the Bible?

*Filter Two:* I compare the impression with what the Bible says. Is it scriptural? What has God said to people in the Bible who faced circumstances like mine?

*Filter Three:* I ask if this impression requires me to break the law or if it will bring harm to myself or those whom my actions affect (see Proverbs 28:4; 1 John 5:17). God's Word never leads us astray or encourages wrongdoing. Rather, it encourages, exhorts, uplifts, and blesses. Anything contrary to this should be carefully scrutinized. I am not suggesting that the Bible doesn't correct our behavior, convict us of sin, or command us to repent. In fact, the

Word will always encourage us to live holy God-fearing lives. But the Bible never leads us down a harmful or dangerous path—not for ourselves or for others.

*Filter Four:* I request input from spiritual leaders, including those in my accountability group, fellow ministers, and my leadership team. If all the answers line up, then I feel fairly confident that this is something the Lord has laid upon my heart.

So in response to the person who says, "God told me to jump off a bridge," I would ask, "How many times has God told you to do that?" Does it have a scriptural basis? Will it break the law or be considered harmful? Would his pastor or spiritual leader be in agreement? Passing such a statement through these filters brings us to an obvious conclusion.

Several years ago, I needed a voice-over talent to introduce my radio show and podcast. There is nothing better to introduce a radio program than a voice everyone recognizes, one that carries weight. But I had no leads and didn't know where to begin. So I prayed.

Late that night, my wife and I were lying in bed watching television when a Geico commercial appeared. In it, a middle-aged blond woman sat behind a table in what appeared to be her kitchen. Behind her, a distinguished-looking bald man stood at a microphone, wearing headphones and dressed in white pants and a yellowish button-down shirt. The narrator announced that she was a real Geico customer and that to tell her story they'd brought in "that announcer guy from the movies."

Perhaps you do not know his name, but you have heard his voice. His name is Don LaFontaine, the most famous movie-trailer announcer in the history of Hollywood filmmaking. As soon as the woman in the commercial finished her first line, the attention switched to him. He repeated what she said but with a dramatic music bed and a rich, deep voice that was immediately recognizable as the one millions of us have heard over the past thirty years.

As soon as I heard his voice proclaim his signature phrase, "In a world," I felt a strong impression in my heart saying, *There's your voice-over talent!*

Somewhat shocked, I thought, *Wow! I'm not sure what I am supposed to do with that.* I didn't know how to respond. Should I call him up and say, "Hi, my name is Jason Frenn. I have a need for a voice-over talent, and after praying, I guess you're supposed to be my voice-over guy"? That not only sounds strange, it sounds a bit crazy. So I just lay there for about thirty minutes. One thing was certain, however, the impression grew. So I got up and Googled the master voice-over talent.

I discovered that Mr. LaFontaine has a nickname in the industry: "the Voice of God." He has recorded approximately five thousand movie trailers dating back to the 1960s. Mr. LaFontaine has lived behind the microphone, sold hundreds of millions of us on seeing movies, and made a great living doing it. Needless to say, it took some guts to call his agent the next business day.

Over the weekend, I talked with some of my closest friends and told them about what I felt I needed to do. None of them thought I would receive a positive response, but no one felt it would hurt to ask.

The next business day morning, I called the agency. The receptionist who answered kindly connected me to the executive assistant, who was gracious enough to allow me to leave a voice-mail with his agent. To this day, no one has returned my call. Am I offended? Not at all. That's Hollywood. Aside from his agent's contact info, though, I found a general e-mail address for Mr. LaFontaine. I seriously doubted whether he would receive my petition. After all, someone that famous would most likely have a personal assistant, publicist, and manager, in addition to his agent, to filter out nonprofit solicitors like me.

The impression, nonetheless, was persistent. I couldn't ignore it.

Was it biblical? It wasn't *non*biblical.

Was it in line with my golden thread? Did it align with the first, second, and third pillars? Yes. The motive behind the request was to promote a radio program to reach people.

Was this something God would ask of me? If He asked me to give up living in the United States for more than seventeen years to serve as a missionary in Central America (which He had done), I believed this request could easily be something God might ask of me.

Was it an illegal or harmful request? Absolutely not.

So in order to satisfy my conscience before the Lord, I composed a letter, thinking to myself, *Well, after I send off this e-mail, it's in God's hands.* The e-mail was simple and to the point. The time stamp on the e-mail was 6:39 p.m., August 31, 2006. The next morning, September 1, at 11:03 a.m., there was an e-mail in my in-basket from him with one sentence. It read, "Jason, send me the copy, and I'll be happy to record it for you.—Don."

I went into shock at that very moment. I must have stared at the computer screen for five minutes, completely bewildered. When the commotion wore off, the true task made itself evident and a sense of urgency hit me. I had to write copy for the king of voice-overs, and I had to do it quick! *What in the world do I say?*

Be careful what you pray for, friend. You just might get it.

I wrote out the copy within five minutes with a nicely worked clause reiterating the fact that I was a minister and that I would need some time, perhaps extended time, to cover his fees. I fired off the e-mail close to noon. At 1:19 p.m., there was another e-mail sitting in my in-basket with an audio file, MP3 attachment. Again, there was one sentence in the body of the e-mail. It read, "Jason, here you go. . . . All the best—Don."

When I asked him what I owed him, he replied, "Nothing." When I asked if I could use the same recording for our television specials, he replied, "No problem. I am happy to lend my voice to your project at no charge."

In the months following, we occasionally corresponded via e-mail, but we never spoke on the phone and never met in person. Don LaFontaine passed away on September 1, 2008, two years to the day after he recorded my radio intro. I am eternally grateful to the Lord for His direction and to Don for his generosity. I encourage you to subscribe to my podcast. It's worth it just to hear his voice!

Lying in bed that night, I received a strong impression that said, "There's your voice-over talent." For a split second, I had serious doubts. But the impression was persistent. It grew. It wasn't contrary to Scripture. It was in line with my golden thread and the three pillars. It didn't violate any laws or harm those involved. Indeed, it was God's voice. Indeed, it was His leading.

Discerning God's voice is a discipline we must practice in order to perfect. It's something that if practiced every day will help us grow to become people who break barriers and overcome all that holds us back. Believe me, friend, this is what God wants for your life. He wants you to hear His voice and become all you're destined to be. Developing the spiritual discipline to discern God's voice will help to cement the third pillar in your life. Hearing God's voice and acting on it will affect every area of your life. Hearing God's voice prepares us for the third discipline, obedience. Talking to God and listening to Him take us only so far as we endeavor to break barriers. Obeying Him completes the journey.

### 3. The Discipline of Obeying God's Will

The difference between those who break their barriers and those who don't is a simple one. Those who listen to God's voice and do what they're told move ahead (see Deuteronomy 28:1–14). They partner with the Spirit, establish the third pillar in their lives, and obey His voice.

God already knows which door will be open before you get there. He is an all-powerful, all-present God who sees everything. He knows everything. He has sovereign control over everything. You can rest assured that if you follow His lead, He will guide you through the maze of life, over the obstacles, and through the storms. So it only makes sense to act when He leads you. The discipline to do so comes from the power of the Spirit.

My wife, Cindee, and I have shared a ministerial vision since 1991: communicating Christ's message of hope to millions of people. When we first started holding open-air meetings, crowds ranged between 400 and 800 people. In the years following, our open-air meetings drew about 1,500 people in nightly attendance. We knew that if we were going to grow and reach entire cities, we would need a strong boost. Indeed, there was a barrier. Actually, it seemed more like a chasm.

So I asked God to help me think outside the box in order to reach more people. I knew that utilizing the media was one of the strongest forms of getting the word out. It's a powerful way to publicize and would help us accomplish what we felt God called us to do as missionaries: reach millions of people. Unfortunately, we had no budget. We had no extra funds for advertising.

Soon a dream emerged in my heart. At first I wasn't quite sure if it was God's solution or some crazy idea I had conjured up.

I felt that the Lord was leading me to contact the largest secular network in the country and ask for an appointment with the owner. Once I had secured the appointment, I would ask for five daily commercial spots—starting ten days before each crusade, announcing the event for the foreseeable future *free of charge*.

As you can imagine, I felt that was a few steps above my level of faith. But I couldn't shake the impression. It grew and grew with each passing day. The more I pondered it, the more I realized it wasn't just my dream. It was also God's. It was a dream that I could no longer keep within me. I couldn't resist it. I had to act on it. I faced a barrier, and I believed God wanted me to break that barrier to reach more people who needed Christ.

Obedience is a decision. It's doing what God wants done when He wants it done. It means that we act in accordance with His wishes and direction for our lives. Being obedient is the act of using the godly strength He's given to do what we know to be good and wise.

That's why the Bible says: "This is what Hezekiah did throughout Judah, doing what was good and right and faithful before the LORD his God. In everything that he undertook in the service of God's temple and in obedience to the law and the commands, he sought his God and worked wholeheartedly. And so he prospered" (2 Chronicles 31:20–21 NIV).

You will never get from point A to point B if you don't follow through on the conviction that you honestly believe God put in your heart. That's all God asks of us. He asks us to be obedient— to follow not some mystical direction, but rather the mission (first pillar) we genuinely believe He has placed before us. This is discipline in its purest form: following through on what we know to be good and wise.

Finally I picked up the phone and called the network. The operator transferred me to the receptionist on the executive floor, who then transferred me to the owner's executive assistant.

The kind and professional voice on the other end of the phone said, "May I help you?" I responded, "My name is Jason Frenn, and I have an idea that is going to be of great benefit to this country and to your network. All I need is fifteen minutes with the owner of the network at your earliest convenience." She responded, "Please fax us your request for an appointment. If there is time, we'll get back to you. But please understand, we are extremely busy." Without hesitation, I faxed in my request for the appointment and waited.

Five days passed before I received a call from the network owner's executive assistant. She said, "In ten days you have fifteen minutes with the owner of the network. Be here at ten a.m." I was more than surprised that they made time for me, but I turned to the Lord and said, "What have I gotten myself into?" His impression was strong: *Don't waver. Remember, ask for five commercial spots—starting ten days before each crusade, announcing the event for the foreseeable future* free of charge.

Ten days passed, and my crusade coordinator and I drove to the network headquarters. After waiting in the reception area for nearly fifteen minutes, we were told to take the elevator to the executive floor. We were escorted to the conference room and left unattended for another ten minutes. The conference room was plush and had a large television screen and media center at one end. The carpeting was steel-gray, the decor was executive, and the crown molding added a classic touch. The burgundy wingback chairs permeated the room with the smell of Italian leather. Needless to say, I felt a bit nervous.

Ten minutes proved to be a long time. Thoughts began to race through my head. *Jason, what in the world are you doing here? Are you nuts?* Does this thinking sound familiar, friend?

If we are going to develop the discipline of obedience, we must be willing to get out of our comfort zones and follow the Lord wherever He leads us. If we are living in accordance with the will of God (pillar one), we can rest assured that God will lead us through! He wants each of us to reach our greatest potential for His glory.

I remembered that the dream in my heart to reach a city was not mine alone. It was God's. Suddenly, the door flew open, and one by one the executives came filing in. Dressed in Italian designer suits, they rounded the corner of the conference table and found their assigned seats. Almost in unison they pulled out their chairs and sat down. An awkward moment of silence settled over the room. After several minutes, the door opened again. This time, it was the owner of the network.

In walked a seventy-five-year-old lady, elegantly dressed. As soon as she entered the room, every man stood as she nodded and went straight to her chair. She sat down, and we all followed suit. Then she looked directly across the table at me and said, "Now, what can I do for you, young man?"

My heart was racing. My forehead was beading with perspiration. It was as though time stood still. That is when I felt that conviction once again: *Tell her that we want five daily commercial spots—starting ten days before each crusade, announcing the event for the foreseeable future* free of charge.

So I looked directly at her, took a deep breath, and said, "I want to thank you for the opportunity you have extended to us to be here. I understand that your time is precious so I will get straight to the point. We believe that God loves this country and He wants us to help as many people as we can." Every executive looked straight at me. There wasn't one distraction in the room. I continued, "In the face of neighborhoods and cities that are being overwhelmed with drug abuse, prostitution, and gang violence, we have a message of hope for those who desire change. Where there is suffering, poverty, and abuse, we have come to proclaim a message of love and healing. And we need you to partner with us to proclaim that life-changing message. I am asking you to grant us five daily commercial spots announcing our open-air events for the foreseeable future . . . uhh." Then I paused for a split second before saying rather quickly, "Free of charge." I pressed my lips together in a slight smile.

About five seconds passed. She never broke eye contact.

During those few moments that seemed like eternity, she looked at me with the most professional poker face I had ever seen. She slowly turned her face and at the last possible second broke eye contact with me, shifting her eyes to her assistant. Then she looked back at me and said, "Well, that seems reasonable to me. Is that *all* you need?" With uncertainty and disbelief I responded, "I believe so."

She said to her assistant, "Well then, give them whatever they need. Now, if you will excuse me, I must attend to some other issues. And oh, by the way, I deeply appreciate and admire what you are doing for this country!" Then she got up and left the meeting.

I was in shock. I was speechless. I didn't know if I should laugh or cry. Was it a dream or a reality? After the door closed behind her, the assistant turned to me and said, "Mr. Frenn, all we need is your commercial spots in a broadcast-quality format, and we'll take it from there. Let us know if you need anything else."

We were about to leave when I stopped. I couldn't leave without finding out why she was so supportive without any objections. So I asked the assistant, "Please tell me something. She never expressed any concerns. She never asked any pointed questions. She expressed no reservations. She said yes, and that was it. Why is that?" The assistant replied, "The owner is in favor of building a spiritual foundation for this country. She believes that people need God's help more than they need unrealistic solutions or broken political promises. Besides, she is very devout in her relationship with God."

I learned a very valuable lesson at that moment. God has agents in every level of society and in every country of the world. He has agents in high places, powerful places, and strategic places. He taps them when it's necessary to fulfill His agenda and criteria. No matter how large your dream, no matter how big your barrier, God has the power and resources to pull it off.

Since 1997, the most powerful secular network in that country has helped us promote our open-air outreaches and granted us commercial spots—starting ten days before each crusade, announcing the event, and they do so *free of charge*.

For me the challenge was learning to obey the Lord in the midst of intimidating circumstances. God wants to help us break barriers, but if we are going to succeed, we must obey Him. Friend, do you have large barriers to break? Are you facing significant challenges? Pray through them, learn to discern God's voice, and obey Him. The Lord will go before you and level the mountains, break down the barriers, and cut through every obstacle in your way (see Isaiah 45:2)! Had I not obeyed the Lord's leading, millions of potential viewers would not have seen those commercial spots. Obedience was essential in order to break a major barrier to reach hundreds of thousands of people.

We've talked about some of the things that you and I can do to build godly discipline in our lives. Now we're going to direct our attention to the One who empowers us to break barriers and become all we are destined to be. Godly discipline, that is, the strength to live a Christian life and overcome the challenges that try to hold us back, comes from the Holy Spirit. This is the final step toward establishing the third pillar in our lives. In the life of the believer, the Holy Spirit gives us the strength to break the barriers!

## UNLEASHING SUPERNATURAL STRENGTH

In Acts 16, the Holy Spirit played a major role in guiding, strengthening, and equipping the disciples. Jesus' words came true. He ascended into heaven and forty days later, the Holy Spirit empowered the disciples (see Acts 2). From that point, the disciples depended on Him for guidance, strength, resistance, and power. The following story shows how Paul and Silas were connected to the Holy Spirit and how He helped them break major barriers and overcome adversity. They firmly established the third pillar in their lives.

One day, Paul and Silas were heading to a place to pray. Along the way, they ran into a slave girl who earned a large amount of money for her masters by telling the future. This girl followed Paul and his friends for more than a week, telling everyone, "These men are servants of the Most High God, who are telling you the way to be saved" (Acts 16:17 NIV). Paul turned around and said to the spirit in her, "In the name of Jesus Christ I command you to come out of her!" (verse 18 NIV). Suddenly, the spirit left her and with it, the ability she had to tell the future. When the owners of the girl found out what had happened and that their good source of income was cut off, they grabbed Paul and Silas and took them to the authorities.

Without due process or trying them as Roman citizens, the rulers had Paul and Silas stripped and beaten. The guards hauled them off and threw them into prison. The jailer was instructed to watch them very carefully, so he placed them in the innermost cell and bound their feet to the wall.

Late that night, they were praying and singing songs to the Lord while everyone listened. All of a sudden, a massive earthquake struck and the prison doors flew open. The chains came out of the wall, and all the prisoners were freed. When the jailer woke up and discovered that everyone was gone, he drew his sword. Just before he took his own life, Paul raised his voice and told him, "Don't harm yourself! We are all here!" (16:28 NIV).

The jailer, full of fear, came to Paul and Silas and asked them, "'What must I do to be saved?' They replied, 'Believe in the Lord Jesus, and you will be saved—you and your household'" (16:30–31 NIV). After Paul shared the good news with him, the jailer and his entire family were baptized.

Paul and Silas had stumbled over one of the greatest obstacles ever. Because of the greed of sinful people, they were branded as lawbreakers. Paul, a Roman citizen, should have been given due process. There were laws guaranteeing him certain inalienable rights. He should have had a fair trial where he could argue his position. Instead, he and those with him were severely flogged and thrown into a maximum-security facility.

Paul and Silas clearly had the third pillar established in their lives. This wonderful passage of Scripture can teach us many things about how the Holy Spirit helps us break our barriers and overcome adversity. He helps us stay strong in the midst of trial and tribulation. Let's look at four powerful lessons from this story.

## 1. The Holy Spirit Guides Us in Our Prayers

When the disciples were in the inner cell with their feet and hands chained to a brick wall, they were unable to shout for help, make a phone call, send a carrier pigeon, or bribe the guard. They were stuck with nowhere to go. The only one they could depend on was the Holy Spirit. The only way for them to find a solution was through the Spirit of God, and He led them to do the only thing they could do: pray and sing. So they turned their hearts toward the Lord, opened their mouths, and began to worship.

The Holy Spirit guides us through the storm, shows us how to pray, and, most important, connects us with a supernatural solution when there doesn't seem to be a way. As the disciples were led to sing and pray, the Holy Spirit responded with exactly what was needed: a miraculous earthquake.

## 2. The Holy Spirit Edifies and Strengthens Us Through Times of Trial

Instead of becoming discouraged, unruly, and rebellious, Paul and Silas focused their hearts on the Lord, and as a result became rejuvenated. Many times, when people face adversity and difficulties, they become discouraged and even depressed. When insurmountable obstacles force us into a corner, we can either run and hide or join forces with the Spirit of God and tap into His guidance. That is what Paul and Silas did. The Holy Spirit led them to sing hymns and pray. As a result, their hearts were encouraged and they were able to sense God's presence in what was a difficult and frightening circumstance. In the same way, when we are filled with the power of the Holy Spirit, the Spirit of God gives us the strength to triumph over spiritual depression.

## 3. The Holy Spirit Helps Us Resist the Devil and Temptation

After the earthquake, they could have escaped from the prison immediately along with all the other inmates. Most people would have run and never looked back. Instead, they did the right thing. The earthquake had turned the facility to rubble. At once, all the prison doors flew open, and everyone's chains came loose. But Paul and Silas didn't move. When the jailer woke up and saw the prison doors open, he took out his sword and was about to take his life. He did this because his superiors would have had him killed for letting the prisoners go free. Notice how Paul reacted. He said, "Don't harm yourself! We are all here!" (Acts 16:28 NIV). The disciples resisted temptation and stayed true to their convictions.

In John 16, Jesus talks about how the Holy Spirit will guide our consciences. Verses 8–11 say, "When he comes, he will convict the world of guilt in regard to sin and righteousness and judgment: in regard to sin, because men do not believe in me; in regard to righteousness, because I am going to the Father, where you can see me no longer; and in regard to judgment, because the prince of this world now stands condemned" (NIV). The Holy Spirit convicts our consciences if we are involved in immoral activities. On the other hand, He also affirms our good behavior as we turn our hearts toward God and aim to fulfill His purpose. He speaks to us through that still, small voice inside each of us that tells us when we are acting correctly or inappropriately.

Why is this so important? Because you must be prepared. Every time you face a barrier, the devil will present you with an easy way out. He will show you a secret way to escape, and you will be tempted, especially if it seems harmless or insignificant. Nothing is more difficult than resisting temptation while facing a great barrier. It is difficult because Satan never lets us see the consequences of our actions until it is too late. We are blinded to the potential repercussions of our behavior. For this reason, people who have fallen into the temptation of an extramarital affair often say, "I had no idea my actions would cause so much pain for the rest of my family."

In most cases, if we fail to stand firm when we are resisting temptation, we will wind up paying a great price. Not twelve hours after the earthquake Paul and Silas endured, the authorities granted them their freedom. Imagine what would have happened if they had fled. If caught, they would have been put to death. Only the discipline of the Holy Spirit will enable you to resist the temptation of easy solutions. Only the strength of the Spirit of God will enable you to live for the godly heart the Lord has created in you.

## 4. The Holy Spirit Gives Us Power to Be Witnesses and Help Others Find Christ

When the jailer was about to take his life, Paul intervened. Paul recognized there was something much more important than his own freedom. The jailer's salvation was hanging in the balance as well.

Paul understood that every barrier is an opportunity to present someone with the gospel of hope. In spite of his exhaustion, he depended on the Holy Spirit for the power to present the jailer and his entire family with the message that Christ had come to set the captives free. When the jailer brought them out and asked, "What must I do to be saved?" they replied, "Believe in the LORD Jesus, and you will be saved—you and your household" (Acts 16:31 NIV). After taking them into custody in his house, the jailer and his entire family were baptized.

In spite of their horrific experience, Paul and Silas went the extra mile to help the jailer and his family. They could do so only because God gave them the strength through the Holy Spirit. When they were thrown into jail, they listened to the Spirit of the Lord and prayed. They depended on the Lord for edification and strength. They resisted temptation and asked the Holy Spirit for the strength to bless a man who was in charge of their incarceration. And indeed, they blessed him and his entire family! They gave him the greatest gift of all.

So get connected to the Spirit! Make the Holy Spirit your best friend. Ask Him for the strength to stay the course through every obstacle you encounter. He guides us, comforts us, and strengthens us to break the barriers that try to hold us back. Building a relationship with Him will firmly establish the third pillar in your life.

He is all-powerful, and He loves us with an immeasurable love. Our ability to break barriers comes when we take hold of the gifts He's so happy to give us. So reach out, friend. Take the gifts He lovingly offers. You have no greater advocate, no greater friend, and no greater fan! He loves you dearly—you are the apple of His eye!

⌒∞⌒

In this chapter, we've learned about three powerful spiritual disciplines that can help us firmly establish the third pillar in our lives, the discipline of the Spirit, which includes the disciplines of prayer, hearing God's voice, and obedience. We also learned that the Holy Spirit is our greatest ally. He guides us in our prayers, edifies us during times of trial, strengthens us to resist temptation, and empowers us to help others find Christ.

As we close this chapter, let's focus our hearts one more time upon the Lord. As you pray this prayer with me, allow the Lord to fill you with His Holy Spirit. Allow Him to encourage you and build His godly discipline in you to break every barrier preventing you from becoming all God has destined you to be.

*Lord, I thank You for Your goodness and wisdom. I recognize that without You I would be lost and overwhelmed in this world. I turn to You at this time and ask for help. Fill me with Your Holy Spirit and allow me to serve You with all of my heart, mind, soul, and strength. Give me the strength to live a disciplined life guided by Your goodness and wisdom. Guide my thoughts and give me the strength to manage my emotions. Help me face temptation with Your strength. Help me face my fears with Your power. Help me to overcome depression and discouragement with Your hope and encouragement. Help me to think in such a way that my self-talk reflects what You feel about me. Most of all, help me to have the mind of Christ.*

*Holy Spirit, help me to redefine pleasure so I can see things as You see them. Help me to find godly pleasures and be bonded to the people and things You have called me to be close to. I want to honor You in all I do. I want to serve You with all my heart. I want to break the barriers, overcome adversity and reach my greatest potential, and glorify You with my life. I ask these things in Christ's name. Amen.*

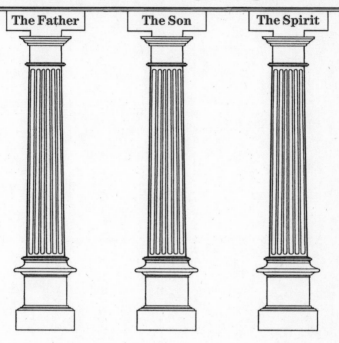

# *You Can Be Who God Wants You to Be!*

THE PURPOSE of this conclusion is to show you how the three pillars of heart, wisdom, and discipline work together to help you break the barriers. It is a summation of all we have learned throughout the pages of this book. My desire, however, is for this to be not merely theoretical but a practical aid to facing everyday challenges.

At the beginning of the book, I said you are not here by mistake—your life is not an accident, nor do you exist because of some random chance through evolution. You are here for a reason. God intends for you to have a meaningful and significant life. That's why you are here.

So let us return to one of the first sets of questions we faced at the beginning of this book. What is the greatest obstacle you face? Is it something that challenges your family? Is it something that challenges your finances? Does it challenge your health? Every barrier, no matter how great or small, requires us to have a godly heart, godly wisdom, and godly strength in order to overcome it.

## PILLAR I: THE HEART OF THE FATHER

My grandmother Afifi Frenn was born in Zahlé, Lebanon, in 1907. After turning sixteen she was sent to Paris, France, by her parents to be married to a distant cousin she had never met. His name was Michael Frenn. After their wedding ceremony, they arrived at the coastal town of Cherbourg, where they boarded an ocean liner called the *Aquitania*. From there they headed to the United States to begin a new life. On October 19, 1923, the ship arrived in New York, where the couple went through U.S. immigration on Ellis Island.

The newlyweds moved to Okmulgee, Oklahoma, and opened a bar and grill. In Oklahoma, my grandmother started going by the name of Eva. They lived there for seventeen years and began to raise seven children in the small Oklahoma town of a few thousand. Living through the Great Depression and the dust bowls of the Great Plains, they endured many trials and tribulations. In 1940, they moved to San Fernando, California, and opened another restaurant. They had two more children after arriving in the Golden State.

In 1945, they moved into a 6,000-square-foot house in North Hollywood. It had five bedrooms, three and a half bathrooms, and a maids' quarters and rested on a full acre of prime San Fernando Valley real estate. Located within ten miles of the restaurant, Universal Studios, the Burbank airport, Hollywood, and downtown Los Angeles, the house was ideal for the Lebanese family of eleven. The children began to adapt well to Southern California culture, and the restaurant was prosperous. Michael and Eva had started a new family in a foreign culture and were beginning to see the fruits of living the American Dream.

In September of the following year, however, tragedy struck the family. Without warning, Michael died of a heart attack, leaving behind a wife and nine children. He was forty-eight. The entire family was devastated and thrown into turmoil. A man who was deeply loved and admired had suddenly slipped into eternity. In a matter of minutes, the entire burden of running a restaurant as well as the financial responsibility for a small business and mortgage payments shifted to Eva. She was left with the overwhelming task of raising all of the children on her own in a foreign culture. At thirty-eight years of age and as a young widow, she was facing one of the greatest barriers anyone could ever imagine.

My grandmother told me of an experience that marked her life forever. It happened shortly after the death of her husband. In a moment of desperation, she needed God more than ever, and God responded. As she was lying in bed, filled with anguish and despair, Christ suddenly appeared to her. He stood over the bed with outstretched arms and said He would help her through the difficulties she was facing. She couldn't utter a word. She simply gazed at Him with tears in her eyes. That day, she made a commitment to follow Him, attend church, and make serving Him a priority in her life.

Indeed, she was faithful to her commitment. From that day forward, she reached out to God and began making the heart of God her own: building the first pillar to break the barriers. Prayer was a daily discipline in her life. Every weekend, my dad would take me to her house, where I would see her spiritual disciplines in action. I remember how she started each day. Immediately after waking up, she would kneel by the side of her bed and dedicate another day to serving the Lord.

Every day she asked God for protection over her house, over her children, and eventually, over her grandchildren. She made God her best friend, and she yearned for His heart to beat within hers. She realized what so many people in this world fail to see: Without God, we are lost. Without God, barriers will overwhelm us and keep us from reaching our greatest potential. Without Him, there is no hope. She also realized that with God, we can break every barrier. With God, we will get to the other side. With God, all things are possible.

My grandmother made attending church a priority. She didn't stay locked inside the four walls of her house. She didn't allow depression to destroy her. Instead, she became one of the most active members in her church. For many years, she went to five or six services a week. Involved in women's ministries and special drives to help the poor, she dedicated hundreds of hours a year to the cause of Christ. She took me to church every Sunday. Rain or shine, when my weekly clock struck Sunday, I was heading to the 10:00 a.m. service. At times it was in Arabic, and I didn't understand much of it. But I learned to appreciate the need to embrace the heart of God and His attributes.

Throughout my life I have observed people who have taken on the heart of God. Among the many who have impressed me, my grandmother was one full of the attributes of God. She embraced His love, joy, peace, patience, kindness, goodness, faithfulness, gentleness, and self-control. As a result of her relationship with Christ, she led the family through one of its darkest hours and managed to raise nine children in the process. She held on to the restaurant another ten years after the death of her husband. After its sale on January 1, 1956, the remaining six children at home helped contribute to the family's finances.

By 1960, most of the children were grown and had moved out of the house. My grandmother then opened a guest home for elderly women. She rented out the extra rooms in her home and provided services to five women who needed a place to live. She bathed them. She cooked for them. She dressed them, walked with them, and at times fed them. Some eventually moved into a medical facility, as their age and physical needs required them to do so. Every time there was a vacancy, however, someone else would rent the available room. For fifteen years she dedicated her life to helping other women find a special place they could call home and grow old in a dignified manner.

Every one of us comes into the world with a flaw that causes us to live for ourselves and desire unhealthy things. Our moral character would be greatly twisted without God's help. For this reason, we need a godly heart—to guide us to become all He has destined us to be. This is imperative because everything we do and say comes from our hearts. Matthew 15:18 says, "The things that come out of the mouth come from the heart, and these make a man 'unclean'" (NIV). The first step in breaking the barriers is to have the correct starting point: a godly heart. This is, in fact, where my grandmother started.

As she faced an overwhelming barrier, she reached out to God and embraced His heart. She turned to Him on a daily basis through prayer and the reading of His Word. But there is more to overcoming adversity than simply asking God for help. We need to begin to act out godly attributes in order for them to become a permanent part of our lives.

This is something we decide to do. We decide to love. We decide to be kind and patient. We choose to think in holy and virtuous ways. We forgive others and live lives full of joy. Decide to do these things. Act them out. As we put these habits into action, they become a part of who we are. Eventually, we become those things we long to be. My grandmother lived out the attributes of God and became who God wanted her to be.

Many people in this world are good. Few are good and wise. Being good unfortunately isn't good enough. Why? Too many people lack wisdom. Although they may have a good heart and display the attributes of God, they lack His insights and perspective. For this reason, it is imperative to build the second pillar in our lives: the wisdom of Christ. Godly wisdom gives us the ability to ensure we are good people, and we are making good decisions that are harmonious with our mission. With godly wisdom based upon the mind of Christ, we judge every decision we make in the light of our godly mission.

## A REAL-LIFE STORY OF WISDOM

Recently, I had a conversation with my good friend Don, whom I've known for more than fifteen years. When I first met him, he sat across the table from me at a meeting that would determine whether or not his church would partner with Cindee and me as missionaries in Latin America. Don made a few brief comments that day. At a table full of ministers, he was the only layperson, and ironically he seemed to make the most sense. I had no idea who he was at the time. Little did I know he was one of the wisest people I would ever meet.

His parents were divorced when he was four years old, and he never had a stable family life. He grew up without a consistent father figure because his mother had been married five times. When

Don turned fifteen, he gave his life to the Lord. After graduating from high school, he and his wife-to-be attended the same junior college, located in the San Joaquin Valley in California, for a year and a half. Both came from poverty. Neither had a healthy role model. Don and Maxine knew they loved each other and wanted to spend the rest of their lives together. So they decided to get married. Don was nineteen.

Three weeks after their wedding, Don was laid off from his job as an apprentice clerk in a local market. The next day, he drove to Bakersfield and applied at another supermarket chain as an apprentice grocery clerk. The starting salary was fifty-seven dollars a week. They hired him on the spot. Financially, he and Maxine faced many challenges. They faced many barriers. For a period of time their diet was reduced to a bare minimum. Their budget allowed only cheap cans of tuna every day for several months. According to Don, Maxine learned every way imaginable to prepare tuna.

As time passed, Don moved up through the organization. His keen insight for financial management and good business sense gave him favor in the eyes of those for whom he worked. He was promoted to department manager and was eventually asked to manage a store when he was just twenty-four years of age. The grocery business was always competitive, and the owners were constantly looking for the right approach to become the best. They were obsessed with excellence and efficiency. The organization was on a continuous quest for quality and sought the services of competent experts and outside management consultants.

The company continued to grow, and one day the division manager retired. The vice president of operations asked Don to take over the division. Don agreed. Under his leadership the division grew and the company continued to open more stores. His territory increased over the next few years. One day, the president and founder of the company died, and operation of the organization was placed into the hands of his two sons.

They hired an outside consulting company to analyze the organization, and the upshot was: the older brother was fired and many midlevel managers began to lose their jobs as well. For a long time, Don was unaffected because he was so important to the company and so successful in his job. But then came the day he was "invited" to an appointment in the main office in Los Angeles. Don knew he was facing a huge barrier and turned to God for help.

At the meeting, he was told: "You are too independent and difficult to control," and they informed him he was being let go after eighteen outstanding years with the company. Don was surprised but not shaken. He displayed godly wisdom by not panicking. Instead, he waited until his boss and the consulting team had finished their statement, then he calmly responded:

"You may think you control my life, but you don't. This simply tells me God has something better for me. God has just used you to push me into His new direction for my life and for my family." Then he shared his testimony with them and graciously said good-bye to a few friends in the main office.

He made the two-hour drive over the Grapevine back to Bakersfield. When Maxine came home that afternoon, she was surprised to see him and asked, "What are you doing home early?"

What could he say? "I got fired," he told her.

Don had always had an interest in building houses, but he had always been too busy with the grocery business to learn how to use a hammer and nails. This seemed the perfect time to go to his stepfather, a builder, and learn.

"I need to learn how to build a house," Don told him. "Why don't we frame one together?" His stepfather agreed. This was a sign of godly wisdom. Don humbled himself to learn from someone who knew more about a particular field than he did. He rolled up his sleeves and gained knowledge from his stepfather.

Two weeks after Don's dismissal, they were about halfway through framing a house. A produce specialist who had been terminated the same day as Don came to the construction site with a message saying the president wanted to talk with him.

The president said, "It was a wake-up call when they fired you. It has enlightened me to see all the mistakes the consultant team made with you and some of our previous employees. As a result I have fired the consultant team." Then he asked Don to be his consultant to see who was unjustifiably fired and who should be asked to return. And, he wanted to know, would Don return to the company full-time as well?

Don responded with patience, calmness, and three conditions. First, he insisted they rehire the produce specialist (the one who delivered the message to Don on the construction site). Don felt it would only be fair to rehire him since he was fired due to his closeness to Don. Second, he had planned a family vacation and wanted time to get away with his wife and kids. "Finally," he said, "I need time to pray about your offer."

He agreed to give his response the following week.

Don began to ask God for direction every morning but never heard a response. His only desire was to do God's will. On the day he had committed to give his answer, he felt a release from the Lord to accept the position. Don thought that going back to work was the right thing to do, and he hoped he could make things right by bringing healing to those who had been wounded by the company's downsizing. He wanted to help restore the organization and turn negative attitudes around.

At the same time, he felt that his future lay in the construction business. So he worked for two years and with a planned transition gave his thirty-day notice to the grocery company. He and Maxine had nothing much in the way of finances to begin a construction company, but God gave them confidence and faith.

Although his termination had come as a surprise, he wasn't shaken. Why? His confidence was in the Lord. Both he and Maxine had been faithful to the Lord with their lives and finances. He had been taught to live on 90 percent of what he made. The other 10 percent belonged to God, no matter what. Even when they ate tuna every day for months, they had paid tithes on every check they received. It never occurred to them not to. As their income increased, they began giving to missions and supporting projects all over the world.

When Don was fired, he said, "God, I have been faithful to You, and I believe You will take care of my family." He felt God would watch over his family because they had been faithful to the Lord. Don could not have imagined God would remove the consultation team who fired him, much less rehire everyone who had been unjustifiably terminated. This taught Don great respect and fear for the Lord.

Don started his construction business full-time on April 1, 1976, at age thirty-nine. Thirty years later it is estimated that he has built more than three thousand homes, fifty-four apartment buildings, several office buildings, and a few fourplexes. Today, Don is one of the most prominent developers in the San Joaquin Valley. He has become a multimillionaire and has put a roof over the heads of tens of thousands of families. He and his wife came from great poverty and scarce resources, surviving on the bare minimum, but because they embraced the wisdom of the Son, they also overcame great barriers. Several years ago they started a family charitable foundation and currently give away one million dollars a year. If you were to ask them what the most important lesson in life has been for their family, they would respond: "Be faithful to God and trust Him."

## PILLAR II: THE WISDOM OF THE SON

I see godly forms of wisdom threaded throughout Don's testimony. Displaying humility, trust, and the ability to learn new ideas and paradigms, he overcame many financial barriers to accomplish what he has today. Don and Maxine are the people God wants them to be.

Godly wisdom is a step above all other forms of common sense. It is the ability to make decisions and have sound judgment based upon God's perspective. As we partner with Christ, we gain His insights into how to overcome the adversities we face. Psalm 111:10 says, "The fear of the LORD is the beginning of wisdom; all who follow his precepts have good understanding" (NIV).

We gain godly wisdom by surrounding ourselves with people who have it. The values of those with whom we spend time have an effect on our lives. If we spend time with those who are wise and who see things from a godly perspective, we will grow in the godly wisdom they have learned. We also gain wisdom by reading Proverbs with the program I outlined in chapter 4. Proverbs is packed full of godly perspective and insight to help us become all God has destined us to be.

As we approach the barriers we face, we need God's point of view and a new paradigm. We need to cast aside the limited perspectives that prevent us from seeing the obvious or not-so-obvious choices. Our mind-sets determine much of how we react to the world around us. For this reason, we need to be freed to think creatively and beyond the confines of the box in which we find ourselves.

As you approach your barrier, ask the Lord for guidance. Prayer is the starting point for attaining God's perspective about any obstacle you face. Then reexamine the barrier, embrace every possible solution, analyze your best options, and consult wise people.

Being good and wise isn't good enough. Many people who are good and wise lack the discipline to break the barriers they face. Godly discipline comes from the Holy Spirit and is necessary to put into practice good decisions based upon godly character. People can be good and recognize what the right course of action is. Few have the energy and discipline to carry it out. For this reason, it is imperative to build the third pillar in our lives: the discipline of the Spirit. Combining all three pillars equips us to break any barrier we might face.

## PILLAR III: THE DISCIPLINE OF THE SPIRIT

To avoid the humid ninety-five-degree Central American weather, we headed back to San José, Costa Rica, from the beach late at night. It had been a much-needed vacation following three solid years of ministry. After spending three nights at a resort, we were on our way home. The girls were asleep, the skies were clear, and traffic was light. The four-hour drive went smoothly until we headed into the most uninhabited stretch of the journey. About a hundred miles northwest of San José, we entered a portion of

Central American jungle. It was about 11:30 p.m. There wasn't a streetlight for miles.

When we came around a bend, I heard what I thought was a gunshot from the bushes on the side of the highway. Within seconds, the rim of the car's left-front tire began to scrape the ground. I pulled over to the side of the road, got out, and looked at the tire. It was completely flat, and nothing separated the rim from the asphalt. The rubber had completely shredded, reduced to a few strands. I was puzzled, especially since it was a new tire with only a few thousand miles on it.

My wife leaned out the window and asked what the problem was. I explained, "I am going to have to pull out the spare and change the tire." As soon as I opened the back of the vehicle, I heard a motorcycle fire up and pull out of the bushes and onto the highway and park about two hundred yards behind us. It appeared the two people on the bike had shot out our tire and were now approaching to rob us.

It was a very dangerous situation. I grabbed the jack, placed it next to the front bumper, peeked my head into the driver's window, and said quietly, without waking our daughters, "Cindee, I don't mean to startle you, but I think we have company. Those guys sitting on the bike caused our flat tire."

Cindee immediately got out of the car, stood by the front bumper, and began to sing songs to the Lord. Meanwhile, I frantically began to change the tire. After slightly loosening the lug nuts, I went to grab the spare. Thankfully, other cars and trucks were now passing, and their presence seemed to keep the bandits on the motorcycle at bay.

Pulling the spare out from underneath the vehicle was the most difficult task of all because I had to crawl on my hands and knees in the pitch black and remove a tire that was anchored to the belly of the vehicle. Car after car and truck after truck continued to pass, and we knew the would-be felons were watching us. The girls were still fast asleep, and Cindee continued to sing and pray.

I rolled the spare over to the left-front tire well and started to crank the jack like the Six Million Dollar Man. Within seconds, the vehicle was high enough to remove the old tire.

On this completely dark and usually deserted stretch of road, something amazing was happening: every time I needed light, a car came over the horizon and lit up my small workspace enough for me to complete each task. The timing of the passing vehicles continued so perfectly, the two robbers couldn't make a move.

I put the lug nuts back on and tightened them by hand while the jack still held the car suspended in the air. Then I lowered the vehicle and pulled the jack out from under the frame. I was going to tighten the lug nuts after putting the jack away, but as soon as I placed the jack in the trunk, the bandits fired up the motorcycle and came straight for us. It was obvious we were on course for a confrontation.

Cindee quickly got back in the front seat. I slammed the trunk and ran to the driver's door. The lug nuts were still not tight, but it didn't matter. By the time I reached the driver's seat, the motor-cycle was within thirty feet of reaching our vehicle. I fumbled to find the ignition, and as soon as I started the car, the bike came to a sliding halt, with its front tire in front of our bumper.

When I looked out the window, the bandits were eighteen inches from my face. Both were dressed in black and wearing black helmets. I froze for a split second, until my wife screamed, "*Go!*" This startled me more than the two guys sitting on the bike! As a matter of fact, when she screamed, I jumped, and my foot slipped off the clutch, causing the car to lunge forward and barrel over their front tire. Before they could pull out a gun, we were moving down the highway again.

A few cars approached in the opposite direction, and one came up behind us. The thieves followed us on their motorcycle for a few hundred yards but suddenly broke off their pursuit. I watched in my rearview mirror as they turned around and headed in the opposite direction. We wobbled with our loose front tire into the next town ten miles down the road, where I finished tightening the lug nuts.

To this day, I am eternally grateful to two people: the Lord and my wife. The Lord put hesitancy in the hearts of the two would-be robbers. He sent one vehicle after another to prevent them from approaching us. This was miraculous. Not only was the timing to keep them away from us impeccable, but it also provided the light I needed to change the tire. When God intervenes as He did that night, it's a miracle. When things seem to be impossible and you are backed into a corner, don't give up. Turn to the Lord, and believe in the God of miracles.

I have admired my wife, Cindee, from the first day I met her. She has a heart filled with the character of God the Father, a mind filled with the wisdom of Christ, and the strength of the Holy Spirit. This night, her first impulse was to open the communication lines with God by praying. Instead of running, crying, or panicking, she chose to turn to the Lord for help. That was a wise move. After spending ten minutes praying, she demonstrated the strength of the Spirit. Instead of freezing as I did, she told me to go. Instead of folding to fear, she helped free our entire family from two strangers whose desire was to steal from and harm us. My wife is exactly who God wants her to be.

## HEART, WISDOM, AND DISCIPLINE

I learned two valuable lessons this night. First, no matter what we face, we need to have the right heart, the right wisdom, and the right discipline-produced strength. One without the others leaves a gaping hole in our quest to break the barriers and overcome adversity. Second, sooner or later we all need the Lord to help us. When our backs are to the wall, we need to depend on the God of miracles.

Having godly discipline is doing what is right in the midst of an emotional storm. It begins with the peace of God. It helps us move away from fear and anxiety. Through valleys and over mountains, through highs and lows and in the face of fear and panic, the discipline of God gives us the strength to consistently implement what we know to be good and wise.

You were created with great purpose and destiny. God loves you and has wonderful plans for your life. He made you with talents and gifts. No one else was made like you. You, my friend, are unique, created by God to reach your greatest potential and give glory to God.

We often change only when the pain of staying the same is greater than the pain of change itself. You have a decision to make. Are you ready for change? Are you ready to break the barriers? Are you ready to break those chains that keep you bound? Are you ready to move on to the greatest potential of your life? I trust that your answer is an overwhelming yes. You can be who God wants you to be! You can break the barriers, overcome adversity, and reach your greatest potential.

In every chapter, I have asked you to pray a specific prayer pertaining to the lessons we have learned. This time, I would like to pray for you. As we conclude this book together, I pray it will be a great guide and asset for you. May it be a powerful tool that you can share with others who need God's help in life. May it help you break every barrier you confront. May you overcome adversity and reach your greatest potential. This is my prayer for you:

*Lord, I thank You for my friends who have read this book. I pray they would be greatly blessed. May Your hand guide their development to break every barrier they face. May they overcome all adversity and become all You have destined them to be. May the love of God surround them, bless them, and may Your face shine upon them. In times of darkness may they see Your light. In times of loneliness may they sense Your presence and warmth. In times of tragedy may they sense Your victory and great purpose.*

*Guide them through every difficulty and create in them a clean heart that reflects every attribute of God the Father. Give them the perspective and the wisdom of the Son so they can see through and around every obstacle. Finally, give them the strength and discipline of the Spirit to put into action everything they know to be good and wise. May You prosper, protect, and bless them with the goodness and riches of the kingdom of heaven. I pray these things believing it is Your divine will to bless them in Christ's name. Amen.*

# About the Author

JASON FRENN comes from what he humorously calls a crazy family. While growing up in a nontraditional home where divorce, alcoholism, and family discord were the norm, he realized he couldn't break the dysfunction on his own. After a Hispanic family invited him to attend church in 1982, he began to reach out to God for help and found the strength in Christ to overcome the destructive patterns that had plagued his family for years. In 1991, he left his corporate position as a highly successful sales representative and began serving in full-time ministry.

After attaining his B.A. in History/Political Science and M.A. in Church Leadership from Vanguard University, Jason and his wife moved to Costa Rica as missionaries with the Assemblies of God. Since that time, he has traveled the world as a missionary-evangelist and conference speaker. Over the years, he has held more than fifty evangelistic citywide outreaches in Latin America and the United States and has spoken to more than 2 million people, with 200,000 making first-time decisions to follow Christ.

Jason is a dynamic speaker and author who uses biblical principles and stirring personal testimonies to inspire audiences all over the world. In addition to the citywide outreaches he holds, he is a highly sought conference speaker for churches, nonprofit organizations, and business audiences. Jason is the founder of Taking It to the Nations and Power to Change International. He hosts a daily live radio program on the Radio Nueva Vida network, with a listening audience of 475,000 people. For more information, visit his Web site: www.frenn.org.